HOW TO BE USEFUL TO THE LORD

WITNESS LEE

Living Stream Ministry
Anaheim, CA • www.lsm.org

First Edition, February 2002.

ISBN 978-0-7363-1577-7

Published by

Living Stream Ministry
2431 W. La Palma Ave., Anaheim, CA 92801 U.S.A.
P. O. Box 2121, Anaheim, CA 92814 U.S.A.

Printed in the United States of America

09   10   11   12   13   14   /   10   9   8   7   6   5   4   3

CONTENTS

PREFACE

This book is composed of messages given by Brother Witness Lee in April and May of 1955 in Baguio, Philippines. It consists of six chapters on how a Christian can become useful in the Lord's hands to accomplish the divine commission in the economy of the grace of God.

CHAPTER ONE

HOW TO BE USEFUL TO THE LORD

THE RELATIONSHIP BETWEEN GOD'S PLAN AND MAN

God is a God with a plan. All of God's work in the universe, from ages past to eternity future, is accomplished according to His plan. This plan must be accomplished through man and also in man. Hence, God wants to gain all His created and redeemed people for the accomplishment of His plan.

Do not think it is an accident that God uses us today. God's use of us is altogether based upon His predetermined plan. Everyone that God uses is within the realm of His plan. Because God's plan is carried out only in man, God has to use man to a very great extent. As long as someone is a citizen of a certain country, he is within the sphere of usefulness to that country and can be used by it. Likewise, we who belong to the kingdom of God are within its realm of usefulness.

THE NEED OF GOD'S CALLING

Everyone who has been saved has the position and the potential to be used by God. God confirms man's usefulness to Himself not only by creating and redeeming man but also by calling him. The reason God created and redeemed man is that He intends to use man. However, as far as man's feeling is concerned, creation and redemption are not enough to convince man that God intends to use him. Therefore, God must also call man to confirm to man His intention to use him. In other words, we may feel that although God has created and redeemed us, He may not necessarily use us. Only when we are clear about God's calling us can we say with assurance that God intends to use us. Therefore, to us God's calling is a confirmation of His intention to use us. Now the question we must ask ourselves is, "Has God called us, and how do we know that He has called us?"

GOD'S VISITATION

We may have the concept that understanding God's calling is a difficult matter. Actually, we only need to ask ourselves if from the day we were saved until now we have ever had the feeling of wanting to be used by the Lord or have ever heard within us a soft, gentle voice saying that the Lord wants to use us. If we have had such a feeling, then we can know that the Lord has called us. For us to have a heart that is willing to be used by the Lord is the result of a tremendous work of the Lord. This work is far greater than the Lord's work of creating us.

The Lord's work of creating us was not as great as His work of putting within us a heart that is willing to be used by Him. His working in man in this way is His greatest way of visiting man. In other words, this work is His coming to man and His visiting with man. How did we get a heart that desires to be for the Lord's use? Previously we did not even care for Him, yet to our surprise we now have the desire to be for His use. This proves that this is the Lord's visitation and that the Lord's grace has come to us.

During the past thousands of years God has come to man and visited man numerous times. Unfortunately, not many in the church today have sensed His visitation. God is always coming to man, yet man often puts Him aside. We should not think that in order to have God's calling we must hear a voice like thunder from heaven or see a great light as Paul did on the way to Damascus (Acts 9:3; 22:6). Actually, in principle, the gentle, small voice within us is no different from the calling that Paul received on the road to Damascus. We may use sunlight as an illustration. Although there is a difference between the intensity of the heat of the dim light seen at dawn and that of the bright rays seen at noon, the sun is one and the same. Likewise, while God sometimes calls man in extraordinary ways, most of the time He comes to man and visits him in an ordinary way. God's visitation of man is the confirmation of God's desire to use man and the beginning of His use of man.

PAYING A PRICE

The Lord's visitation marks the beginning of God's use of man. Without the Lord's visitation, we have no way to be called. Thus, it is the Lord's responsibility to visit us. However, the Bible shows us that while the Lord has the responsibility of visiting, we also have a responsibility—the responsibility of paying a price (Matt. 8:19-22; 16:24-27; Luke 9:59-62). Moses and David in the Old Testament and Paul and Peter in the New Testament were those who paid a price through the Lord's visitation. When the Lord met Paul on the road to Damascus, He did not immediately give him power, revelation, or gifts. Rather, the Lord told him to enter into the city and let a little disciple called Ananias tell him in just a few sentences what he had to do (Acts 9:5b-6, 10-17). Because Paul was willing to pay this price, he was greatly used by the Lord (Phil. 3:7-8). On the one hand, the Lord always visits man, but on the other hand, man must always pay a price. Therefore, our being useful to the Lord begins with His visitation but also depends on our willingness to pay a price.

The price one has to pay after answering the Lord's call is limitless. No one can say that he has fully paid the price and that there is nothing more to pay. Not even the apostle Paul could say this. Instead, he was always forgetting the things which were behind and stretching forward to the things which were before, pursuing toward the goal, until one day he even gave up his life (vv. 12-14; 2 Tim. 4:6-8). When Paul wrote 2 Timothy chapter four, he had already paid almost all that he could have paid, yet he was still pressing on. All of us have been visited by the Lord, and the visitations we have received were the same. However, due to the differences in the price that each of us has paid, our usefulness in the Lord's hands may differ from one to another. Because Paul paid a greater price than others, his usefulness was also greater than that of others.

Some might say that the Lord has mercy on whom He wills (Rom. 9:18). However, this word was spoken in regard to

Gentiles, such as Pharaoh who had not yet been visited by God (vv. 15-17). We who have been saved by grace have already received the Lord's visitation (Eph. 2:4-5, 8). Therefore, now the question is not whether we have received the Lord's visitation but whether we are willing to pay a price. Our usefulness in the Lord's hands altogether depends on the price we pay. If we pay a big price, our usefulness will be great; if we pay a small price, our usefulness will be limited.

Throughout the years the Lord's visitation has not been rare, yet the Lord is constantly groaning because the price we are willing to pay is too small. This is why the Lord's work today can only advance slowly and the Lord still cannot come back. The Bible shows us clearly that the Lord is waiting for man to pay a price and be used by Him by answering His call. In Isaiah 6:8 the Lord said, "Whom shall I send? Who will go for Us?" We may not have a deep enough understanding of this word. This word implies that the Lord has a great heart's desire in the universe and that He is waiting for man to answer His call. He intends to work in every age, yet there is a shortage of people who are willing to pay the price and answer His call. Whenever there is someone on earth who is willing to pay the price and answer the Lord's call, the Lord will surely use him. The extent of man's answer determines the extent of the Lord's use of man.

THE SCRIPTURAL SIGNIFICANCE OF "GOING UP TO A MOUNTAIN"

The first person in the Bible to "go up to a mountain" was Noah. He arrived at the mountains of Ararat by being in the ark and passing through the flood (Gen. 8:1-5). The emphasis of the judgment by the flood was not on judging sin but on judging the God-offending world. Noah's going up to a mountain symbolizes his being delivered from the judgment and escaping all the situations of rebellion against God. When he reached the mountain, all the situations of rebellion toward God were over. Therefore, in the Bible going up to a mountain to be before God firstly indicates deliverance from rebellion. Although the whole world had fallen into a state of rebellion against God, those who went to the mountain with Noah came out of the rebellion. Secondly, it indicates ascension to the heavens through death and resurrection. Because Noah had been delivered from rebellion and had gone through the flood—a type of the experience of death and resurrection—he entered into a new age to represent God's authority on earth. The significance of Noah's going up to a mountain is the same as all those who would go up to a mountain after him. Every time God leads someone up to a mountain, His intention is that this person would be delivered from rebellion and would pass through death and resurrection to enter into a situation of representing God's authority on earth. This is a summary of the significance of man's experience of going up to a mountain.

In the Bible there is another aspect of the significance of going up to a mountain—one goes up to a mountain for revelation. In many such instances, from Abraham's going up to Mount Moriah (Gen. 22:1-2) to John's being on the island of Patmos (Rev. 1:9; 21:10), the emphasis given to these experiences in the Scriptures is the receiving of revelation. Abraham's going up to Mount Moriah was originally for consecration, but in the end it was for revelation. By going up to a mountain Abraham came to know God as Jehovah-jireh and to know God's work on earth, because God's promise to Abraham was concerning the work He would accomplish on earth. Following Abraham, Moses and Elijah also received revelation when they went up to a mountain (Exo. 19:20; 1 Kings 18:42). In the New Testament the Lord's bringing His disciples up to a mountain was also for revelation (Matt. 5:1). Finally, John's being brought up to a mountain when he was on the island of Patmos was especially for receiving revelation. In John's experience of going up to a mountain we see the ultimate significance of this matter—being delivered from rebellion, passing through death and resurrection, representing God's authority on earth, and receiving an exceedingly mysterious revelation.

The fact that one must go up to a mountain to receive revelation indicates that the receiving of revelation requires the paying of a price. In other words, to go up to a mountain is to pay a price. The Lord's teaching on the mountain in

Matthew 5—7 came after His teaching in the synagogues (4:23) and was also apart from His teaching in the synagogues. The teaching in the synagogues was common, general, and heard by a great number of people. However, after teaching in the synagogues, the Lord brought His disciples to the mountain. The teaching on the mountain was the teaching concerning the kingdom of the heavens; this teaching was high, specific, and heard only by a few who came to the Lord by following Him up the mountain. To go up to a mountain is to pay a price and come to the Lord by drawing near to Him. Throughout the generations very few have been able to understand the teaching in Matthew 5—7, because very few have been willing to pay a price.

If we want to receive revelation, we must determine to willingly pay a price, and we must also draw near to the Lord within. These are the basic requirements for us to have the experience of going up to a mountain and for us to receive revelation. It was by fulfilling such requirements—paying a price and drawing near to the Lord—that Abraham, Moses, and the Lord's disciples were able to receive revelation. It was especially so in the case of John on the island of Patmos; he received the revelation while he was paying a price and drawing near to the Lord on the Lord's Day (Rev. 1:10). We all should learn this lesson.

THE PRICE IN THE GOSPELS— LEAVING ALL TO FOLLOW THE LORD

The Gospels mention numerous times that the Lord called different ones. Strictly speaking, the Lord's calling is not mainly for people to be saved but for people to follow Him. For example, there are Scripture verses such as, "Come after Me" (Matt. 4:19), "Follow Me" (9:9), "Sell your possessions...and come, follow Me" (19:21), "Follow Me, and let the dead bury their own dead" (8:22), and "No one who puts his hand on the plow and looks behind is fit for the kingdom of God" (Luke 9:62). These verses show us again and again how great is the price that must be paid by those who desire to follow the Lord.

In the Gospels the Lord's unique requirement for those

called by Him was that they forsake all their possessions (14:33). This was how the early disciples were called to follow the Lord. For example, Peter said, "We have left all and followed You" (Matt. 19:27). *All* means "everything." If a person with five thousand dollars gives five thousand, and another one who has fifty thousand dollars gives fifty thousand, then both paid everything they had as the price. In the Lord's eyes, both of them have paid the same price. One day the Lord praised the widow who cast two lepta into the treasury, because she had cast in all that she had, even her whole living (Mark 12:42, 44). Therefore, for us to pay a price does not necessarily mean that we spend the most but that we cast in everything we have. One who casts in everything is one who pays a price. The Lord never counts how much we pay. Instead, what He counts is whether we have paid all.

The "all" required in the Gospels is all that we have, including our parents, wives, children, brothers, sisters, houses, businesses, academic degrees, positions, fame, preferences, ambitions, and lives. All of these items are the price that is required in the Gospels. Many of us today, however, have not completely severed our relationships with our relatives. This does not mean that we should outwardly cut off all human relationships. Rather, it means that we should cut off all emotional ties. In short, the Lord wants us to leave all that we have. This is the most severe demand He has of us.

Whenever we touch the Lord, He will demand something from us. This will always be the case. The Lord is never satisfied with the price we have already paid. Whenever He touches us, He will ask us for something. We experience the Lord's most evident presence when He is requiring something of us. On our side, the only time that we will not sense that He is demanding something of us is when we have lost our fellowship with Him. On the Lord's side, His demand upon us will cease only when the new heaven and new earth are established.

Today is the time for the Lord to use man and to gain man to do His work. Hence, He is continually requiring something of us, and His requirements are becoming greater and greater. At first the Lord's requirements are small, but gradually His requirements become greater, deeper, and more severe. If we try to suppress the feeling that He is requiring something, we will suffer a great loss because our fellowship with Him will be interrupted. After a long period of time, the Lord will no longer have a way in us, and consequently, He will be forced to turn to someone else. However, if we consent to His demands, learn to obey, and are willing to pay the price, our feeling will become more and more sensitive, even to such an extent that almost all day long we will have the feeling that the Lord is asking something of us.

If we do not go along with His demands and are not willing to pay a price, then there will be two results. First, on our side, we will be like the young man who went away sorrowing (Matt. 19:22). Second, on the Lord's side, the Lord will not be able to manifest our usefulness to Him. For this reason, we would rather be wrong trying to obey than disobey altogether, and we would rather obey too much than obey too little. If we answer the Lord's requirements, there will also be two results. First, we will be full of joy, and second, the Lord will be able to manifest our usefulness.

We must realize that the basic requirement to being used by the Lord is to consent to His demands. A person who consents to His demands can be used by the Lord even though he may not have a great deal of knowledge of the truth. He can still be used by the Lord even though he may not pray very frequently. The power we gain by paying a price to answer the Lord's demands is often greater than the power we receive through numerous prayers. The power we receive by paying a price to answer the Lord's demands is often greater than the power we receive through the outpouring of the Holy Spirit. People pay attention to the outpouring of the Holy Spirit, yet they do not see that on the day of Pentecost those who received the outpouring of the Holy Spirit had paid a great price. They had left everything to be in the upper room in Jerusalem and had prayed steadfastly in one accord (Acts 1:13-14).

Many people would like to receive the power brought in through the outpouring of the Spirit, yet they are not willing to learn the lesson of paying a price. Hence, they carry out many works, yet their works cannot last and do not have a lasting effect. If a worker wants his work to remain and to last a long time, he must learn the lesson of paying a price. How much the work can remain depends on how much the worker has learned this lesson. The power for doing the Lord's work lies in one's learning this lesson, and in order to learn this lesson, one must pay a price. A person's usefulness before the Lord is based upon how much of a price he has paid before the Lord. We all admire how useful people such as Paul and Peter were to the Lord, yet we neglect the fact that they paid a great price before the Lord. If we are not useful to the Lord today, the only reason is that we are not willing to pay a price, not willing to answer His demands, and not willing to forsake our reputation, our education, our position, our future, and our whole life. Hence, we do not sense the presence of the Lord, we rarely contact Him in fellowship, and naturally, we have little usefulness before Him.

THE PRICE IN PHILIPPIANS—
GIVING UP ALL THINGS TO GAIN CHRIST

The price in Philippians 3 is different from the price in the Gospels. The price in the Gospels refers to all that we have, whereas the price in Philippians 3 refers mainly to all the things that enable us to serve the Lord. For example, *all things* in Philippians 3 denotes our abilities in service (v. 8). We may have the ability to serve, to preach, to testify, and to visit the saints. We may also have eloquence and experience. All these things are included in the price required of us in Philippians 3. The revelation in Philippians 3 is that we should pursue the experience of Christ and the power of His resurrection (v. 10). Therefore, we need to pay the price by giving up all that we have—our theology, eloquence, doctrines, knowledge, and experience—in exchange for Christ, the experience of Christ, and the gaining of Christ. Paul forsook all things that he might gain Christ (v. 8). In other words, he forsook all his abilities in the service of God that he might gain Christ as his ability. We need to cast aside our ability, our eloquence, our doctrines, and our messages and let Christ be our ability, our eloquence, and our message. Only by paying a price in this way will we be able to gain Christ.

Let us use the matter of visiting the saints as an illustration. Since we have gone out frequently to visit the saints, gradually we have learned something concerning this matter. Therefore, we may think that we are experienced in this matter. However, if we do not give up our experience in the matter of visitations on account of Christ, we will not be able to experience Christ through the visitations. Because we want to retain our ability, Christ has no chance to come in. However, if we go to visit the saints by putting aside our experience, then we are no longer depending on our ability. Our ability to visit the saints, which was a gain to us, we have counted as loss on account of Christ. Although we have the ability, we give it up and count it as refuse. In exchange we gain Christ and experience Christ.

The price in Philippians 3 is not a price experienced in a Christian's initial stage. The price experienced in a Christian's initial stage is the price in the Gospels. The price in Philippians comes after the price in the Gospels. One who has not paid the price in the Gospels cannot pay the price in Philippians 3. The price in the Gospels does not require any qualifications—it is the initial price, whereas the price in Philippians 3 requires certain qualifications. Only when a person has paid the price in the Gospels will he be able to serve in Acts, and only when a person is serving in Acts will he have the experience and qualification to pay the price in Philippians 3.

After paying the price in the Gospels, a person will have numerous experiences in the service of God. However, if he stops there, holding on to those experiences rather than giving them up, eventually he will not have any fresh experiences and will therefore be unable to have more experiences of Christ. Hence, Paul said that we should forget the things which are behind and stretch forward to the things which are before (Phil. 3:13). Regardless of how good our past experiences were, they are the things which are behind and have to be forgotten (cf. vv. 5-6). If we preached the word once and saved three thousand, still have to forsake that experience and count it as refuse that we may gain the living Christ. Unless we are willing to forsake our past experiences, we will not be able to have a fresh experience of Christ, and without a fresh experience, we will not have new usefulness in service. There are some whose usefulness before the Lord is old—not fresh and living, because they are not willing to pay the price referred to in Philippians 3 and are therefore short of the experience of Christ and the power of His resurrection.

The price in Philippians 3 may be likened to Abraham's offering of Isaac on the altar (Gen. 22:1-2). Abraham had received Isaac as a promise from God, yet he still had to offer Isaac back anew. Likewise, we still need to offer to the Lord the lessons that we have learned before Him in the past. This is the price in Philippians 3, which is a higher price. The price in the Gospels is paid by a follower of the Lord in the initial stage of his experience. The price in Philippians is paid by one who has already been serving the Lord to a certain extent and has a considerable amount of knowledge of the Lord, a considerable measure of spirituality, a considerable degree of obtainment, and a considerable amount of experience. At this time, the price revealed in Philippians 3 will require him to give up all these "considerables," that is, to give up *all things.* Although these things are good and are "Isaacs," they are all things of the past. Therefore, he has to forget them and pay them as the price so that he may have some new experiences. Only by this can he have a fresh and living usefulness in service.

THE PRICE IN REVELATION—BUYING THREE THINGS

Another place in the Scriptures that mentions the paying of a price in a very clear way is Revelation 3:18. There it mentions buying three things: gold refined by fire, white garments, and eyesalve. These are all matters related to a price. Furthermore, it is the Lord who asks us to buy.

Gold signifies God's nature, God's element. In the church in Laodicea there was much clay but very little gold. In other words, in their midst there were too many things that were outside of God, and there was too little of the element of God. Therefore, the Lord counseled the believers to buy gold. With regard to white garments, the color white denotes purity, the absence of mixture, and garments refer to our walk and conduct. Hence, white garments signify a walk and conduct expressing the purity of God. Third, eyesalve is for anointing the eyes. When the eyes have an ailment and are unable to see, there is the need to buy eyesalve to cure the eyes and make them bright again. In normal situations, the inner nature of a Christian should be pure, and his outward living should be white and bright. All these items require us to buy, to pay a price. God's intention is to accomplish His eternal purpose through man. Thus, after the Lord calls us, we need to pay a price so that we may become useful to Him.

CHAPTER TWO

LEARNING TO PAY THE PRICE
IN OUR DAILY LIFE

THE REAL PURSUING TAKING PLACE
IN OUR DAILY LIFE

At one time or another, we all have made up our mind to pursue spiritual growth and usefulness to the Lord. However, pursuing by our own determination often can become a matter of formality and therefore become inconsistent with reality. Real pursuing should be carried out in every aspect of our daily life. You can be enjoying the sights of mountains and rivers in your travels yet still be pursuing. You can be chatting with a friend about all sorts of topics yet still be paying a price. We should be paying a price and pursuing the Lord in every aspect of our daily life.

We cannot find that the Lord ever presided over a formal meeting while He was on the earth, because the Lord was not bound by formalities. Rather, He led the disciples to pursue in their daily life. Even while they were traveling, they were still pursuing (Matt. 5:1; 8:23; 9:10; 13:1-2, 10, 36; 16:13; 17:1-2; 24:1-3). In the Old Testament Gideon and his followers were tested in their daily life in the matter of how they drank water (Judg. 7:4-8). This should be the principle of our spiritual pursuit. We should not pray only when we enter into a certain room, nor should we preach and work only when we enter into the meeting hall and step onto the platform. If we pray, preach, and work only at these times, we are merely keeping religious formalities.

We can pursue at any time, whether we are on the mountain or by the seashore, on the road or at home. It is in our daily living that people can detect whether we are truly seeking after the Lord and whether we can truly be used by the Lord. If we cannot work for the Lord in our daily life, then we surely cannot work for Him at scheduled times. A true worker is one who is able to render spiritual help and spiritual supply to others in his every move and action during the course of his ordinary daily life. Only this is reality. Our living must be real and not religious. All the persons and things we contact and encounter every day, at every time, and in every place are opportunities for us to pay the price and pursue being useful to the Lord.

A BASIC PRICE TO PAY

A basic price we need to learn to pay in our daily pursuit is that the younger ones must receive help from the older ones, and the older ones must try their best to help the younger ones. In order to become manifested before the Lord as those who are truly pursuing spiritual growth, we must take care of these two matters. On the one hand, we should do all we can to receive help from whoever can render us help, and on the other hand, we should do all we can to help whoever needs our help. This is real pursuing. However, usually our situation is that the younger ones seek out the younger ones while the older ones seek out the older ones. This is neither true pursuing nor paying the price. This is most likely due to our own preference. Always seeking out those who are of your age group in order to talk intimately with them is not paying a price but having your preference. This practice of spending time only with those whose taste and temperament are the same as yours should be torn down. It is due to an unwillingness to pay the price that the younger ones do not go to the older ones. It is also due to an unwillingness to pay the price that the older ones do not go to the younger ones. This kind of situation is mostly caused by being in the flesh and being unwilling to deny the self.

In chapter one of Song of Songs, the seeker pursues the Lord but still has to pasture the young goats (v. 8). If we neglect the young ones, we are not very useful to the Lord. The older ones should go to help the younger ones because they sense the responsibility to do so. The younger ones should go to the older ones because they sense the need to receive help. This is the proper service.

We should not wait until the meeting time to serve. Instead, we should serve while we are working in the office, while we are doing chores at home, and even while we are away from home, traveling during our leisure time. This may be likened to the fact that whether a mother is at home or away from home—working at a job, taking care of some business, or doing some recreational activities—she cannot forget her children. The real lessons of pursuing are learned in our daily life, and the real time to serve is during ordinary times.

KNOWING AND KEEPING OUR POSITION

In the church life no one is solely a younger one or solely an older one; rather, everyone is a younger one and an older one as well. In spite of this, everyone still has to know his position and keep his place. In the work, in the church, and even when we all gather together, the younger ones should behave as younger ones, and the older ones should behave as older ones. Each one should firmly keep his proper position and pay the price to learn this.

Every matter in the universe has certain principles. For example, no one who loses his proper position can be blessed. Anyone who leaves his position will surely lose the blessing that rightfully belongs to him. In the family, the more the children conduct themselves properly as children, the more firmly they stand in their position as children, and the more the parents conduct themselves properly as parents, the more firmly they stand in their position as parents. The same is true in the church—the more the saints grow in a normal way, the more firmly they keep their position. The Bible says that the younger ones should be subject to the older ones (1 Pet. 5:5) and that the older ones should take care of the younger ones (cf. vv. 1-3). We all should know our position without waiting for others to give commands or depending on others to make arrangements. We should always keep our position, paying the price to learn this lesson.

Every person should know his position clearly. For example,

a person who has truly learned this lesson and knows his position would not dare to say anything about the food placed in front of him, regardless of how bad the food is. Even if the food is poisonous, all he would do is refrain from eating it. He cannot say whatever pleases him because he does not have the position to say anything, nor is it the proper time to say anything. A person who has truly learned this lesson will make every effort to speak when it is the proper time to speak. However, if it is not the proper time to speak, he will keep silent. A person who has truly learned this lesson always keeps his position. When it is the proper time to discuss something in a meeting, he speaks. However, outside of the meeting after the discussion is over, he refuses to speak. Knowing our position and keeping our position—this is to pay the price to learn this lesson.

We must always learn to pay the price because only then can we be useful in the Lord's hand. When we all come together, the position of the younger ones and the position of the older ones should be clearly manifested. The more evident this situation is, the more blessing there will be. In the church the more evident the order is, the stronger the church is. The younger ones should not feel ashamed, and the older ones should not feel proud. We should not think that those who correct us are ill-treating us. We should realize that the younger ones' being able to listen to the older ones is a very glorious and sweet thing. Our position is to obey the more advanced brothers and the elderly sisters, whether they are right or wrong. We have no position to say anything before them. Once we say anything in a loose way, we lose the blessing.

Noah committed a grave mistake when he became drunk and uncovered himself. However, when Ham, the father of Canaan, spoke about it, he lost the blessing (Gen. 9:20-27). When there is loose talk in the church, the blessing is lost. Do not think that speaking a few words is a small thing; actually, a small spark can cause a great fire. In our daily life we need to learn the lesson of knowing our position. This requires us to pay a considerable price.

TWO ASPECTS OF THE PRICE

The price we must pay has two aspects. One aspect concerns our inner sense, and the other aspect concerns the light of the truth given to us by the Lord. Ordinarily, what we sense within is mostly related to trivial matters. The significant, rich, and profound things are mostly found in the truth. The latter aspect is seen mostly in the Gospel of Matthew. Matthew is a book concerning the kingdom. The kingdom has a twofold significance in relation to us. On the one hand, it involves the ruling of the heavens, and on the other hand, it requires the paying of a price. Nearly the entire book of Matthew is concerning the requirement of paying a price. However, the most important chapters are five through seven, thirteen, and twenty-four and twenty-five.

Matthew chapters five through seven, consisting of the teaching given on the mountain, concern the reality of the kingdom. Chapter thirteen, consisting of the parables spoken beside the sea, concerns the appearance of the kingdom. Chapters twenty-four and twenty-five, consisting of the prophecies spoken on the Mount of Olives, concern the manifestation of the kingdom. Both the reality and the manifestation of the kingdom were spoken on a mountain. This was because only those who "go up to the mountain" can participate in the reality of the kingdom today and enter into the manifestation of the kingdom in the future. Although a multitude of people followed the Lord, only a small number of them heard the word concerning the reality and the manifestation of the kingdom. Those who heard were those who followed the Lord up to the mountain and who came near to Him. In other words, they were those who paid a price and had fellowship with the Lord. The word concerning the appearance of the kingdom was given beside the sea, which signifies the world usurped and corrupted by Satan. Those who are in the world can only hear the word concerning the appearance of the kingdom. They cannot see the reality and manifestation of the kingdom because they have not paid the price by going up to the mountain and coming to the Lord.

Although the teachings covered in these three sections of

Matthew differ in their content, they have one point in common. In every section there is the requirement that a price be paid. In Matthew 5—7 the price required of us is that our whole being and entire human living be completely given to the Lord, so that we may attain to the surpassing righteousness, enter the narrow gate, and walk on the constricted way. Matthew 13 requires us to be delivered from the great tree and the leaven and to be the wheat and mustard seed. It requires us to be ground and crushed so that we may give the life supply to others. Chapter thirteen also requires us to be the treasure (including the precious stones) and the pearl. In other words, this chapter requires us to pass through the burning of the Holy Spirit and the pressure of sufferings so that we may be valuable before the Lord. In chapters twenty-four and twenty-five the price that we are required to pay has two aspects—the aspect of life and the aspect of work. The aspect of life is that we need to buy the oil, and the aspect of work is that we need to be faithful. To buy the oil—the aspect of life—is to forsake all outward things in our daily life and to care only for the indwelling Spirit. To be faithful in the aspect of work is to use the gift that we have received to supply others.

THE RELATIONSHIP BETWEEN PAYING A PRICE AND RECEIVING SALVATION

We all know that God's salvation consists of two parts. In the first part we receive forgiveness of sins and the eternal life by faith, and in the second part God intends to work Himself into us that we may be mingled with Him as one. The prerequisite to receiving the first part of God's salvation is faith. Strictly speaking, the prerequisite to receiving the second part of God's salvation is the paying of a price. Because God's salvation consists of these two parts, there are two requirements for receiving these two parts. To receive forgiveness of sins and obtain eternal life, it is enough just to have faith. However, if we want God to work Himself into us and mingle with us, we must fulfill the second requirement—we must pay a price.

THE SIGNIFICANCE OF PAYING A PRICE

To pay a price is to put aside everything that is apart from God in order to receive the second part of God's salvation. We must forsake everything that is outside of God, including our self, flesh, natural being, disposition, family, religion, wealth, reputation, position, and future. The totality of all these things that we need to forsake is the "all...possessions" mentioned by the Lord in Luke 14:33 and the "all things" mentioned by the apostle in Philippians 3:8. The Lord said that we need to forsake all our possessions to follow Him, and the apostle said that we need to suffer the loss of all things to gain Christ. We must do this because God in Christ intends to work Himself into us so that we may be united and mingled with Him. We need to forsake, to put aside, everything apart from God, regardless of whether those things are good or bad, in the past or in the future.

Thus, the price we must pay has many aspects, such as the price required in Matthew 5—7, 13, and 24—25, the price in Philippians 3, and the price in Revelation 3:18. In addition, there is also the price related to reward and punishment (1 Cor. 3:8, 14-15; 9:18, 24-25; Heb. 10:35). All these prices involve one principle—the price that we must pay is the loss of everything outside of God. We must put aside everything that is not in agreement with God and that opposes God, replaces God, and is a substitute for God. Otherwise, we do not allow God the adequate opportunity and sufficient ground to freely work Himself into us. As a result, we will not experience God richly.

Do not think that it is too much that the Lord told us to forsake everything. Also do not think that to abandon all things, as the apostle said, is too difficult. The Lord and the apostle said this because in order to experience and obtain God, we must forsake all that is other than God, that is, we must abandon all things. This is not merely a condition, it is a necessity. If we live by ourselves, God cannot be in us as our life. If we rely on numerous persons, things, and matters and do not commit ourselves wholly to God, He cannot be everything within us. If our families, husbands or wives, and children are sweeter to us than God, then God cannot be everything within us. If our education, fame, position, and future are more lovable to us than God, then God cannot be our inner enjoyment and constituent.

Suppose that although we believe in God, we live by things that are outside of God, and these things are everything to us. Although there is no question that we are eternally saved, God's intention to work in us, to the extent that we are completely mingled with Him as one, is absolutely impossible and unattainable. When we live this way, not only have we not fulfilled what is required of us, but also God's intention cannot be attained in us. We have not paid the price, and paying the price is the requirement for God to work Himself into us and be mingled with us.

Some may say that in speaking about paying a price we despise the effectiveness of the Lord's salvation. Those who say this do not realize that what they say is not according to the truth. The part of salvation concerning forgiveness of sins and the receiving of eternal life can be obtained by faith alone. However, if we want God to come into us and be mingled with us, so that He can operate in us both the willing and the working (Phil. 2:13) and enable us to live Christ (1:21a)—always allowing Christ to be magnified in our body (v. 20b)—then we must pay a price. We cannot arrive at this stage merely by faith. We cannot find a verse in the entire Bible telling us that we can obtain this result merely by faith. Paul said explicitly that since God operates in us both the willing and the working, we must obey with fear and trembling (2:12). He also said that if we desire to live Christ, we must not care for whether we live or die. Not only so, if we want to gain Christ and know Him and the power of His resurrection, we need to suffer the loss of all things and count them as refuse (3:8-10). Is this not the paying of a price? The second part of God's salvation requires us to pay a price. This is both a requirement and a fact.

THE PURPOSE OF PAYING A PRICE

The purpose of paying a price is to afford God the opportunity to do in us what He intends to do. The significance of paying a price is that we allow God to have a place in us so that He may come into us to be our life and even to be fully mingled with us without any hindrance, limitation, or difficulty. Our living, preference, inclination, future, and interest must be given up in exchange for Christ because Christ wants to replace everything that we have. We need to hand over all that we have. If we hand over more, we will receive more. If we hand over less, we will receive less. If we hand over nothing, we will receive nothing. If we hand over everything, we will receive everything. We must pay the price and deny ourselves, forsaking our family, career, and future and discarding everything that replaces God. In this way God will come into us to be our life, power, nature, and content.

If someone believes in the Lord yet is not willing to pay a price to gain Christ, then the salvation he receives will consist only of the forgiveness of sins and the receiving of eternal life. The aspect of salvation that includes forgiveness of sins and the receiving of eternal life has been prepared by God for you, and all you need to do is to receive it. However, for God to be mingled with you, you must forsake all that you have. Hence, Matthew says that we need to buy the oil (25:8-9), and Revelation says explicitly that we need to buy gold, white garments, and eyesalve (3:18). The word *buy* in these two passages was spoken by the Lord Himself. Paul did not use the word *buy;* instead, he said, "I have suffered the loss...that I may gain..." (Phil. 3:8). In principle, suffering loss and buying both involve paying a price. The extent of your suffering loss determines the extent of Christ's coming into you. If you hold on to what you already have, you have no way to gain Christ.

The early Christians sold all that they had for the Lord's sake (Acts 2:44-45; 4:32). They once had been under the usurpation of those things, and God therefore had no opportunity, no ground, and no way in them. However, eventually they realized that all those things should not be the goals of their pursuit but that God Himself should be their unique goal. Hence, they hated all those things and suffered the loss of them. The rich young man in the Gospels loved the Lord and wanted to follow the Lord, yet eventually he went away sorrowing (Matt. 19:16-22). Why did he go away sorrowing? It was because he would not sell his possessions. Since he was usurped by all those things, Christ had no place in him.

Whenever a person is usurped by his reputation, future, position, power, and relatives, there is no way for Christ to have the first place in him. The Lord said that no one can serve two masters (6:24). This means that no one can have two loves. This matter cannot be resolved merely by faith. Therefore, at the end of the Gospel of John, a book that frequently refers to faith (1:12; 3:15-16, 18, 36; 6:40; 20:31), the matter of love is mentioned. Many Bible readers acknowledge that John 21 was added by the author as an afterthought. The Gospel of John obviously concludes with chapter twenty, yet the writer added another chapter—chapter twenty-one, which is of another nature. The first twenty chapters of John speak about faith, but the last chapter, chapter twenty-one, speaks about love (vv. 15-17). Peter and John had no problem with the matter of faith. However, unless they left their fishing boats and nets, they could not gain Christ. Today there are so many believers who are in John 20, but how many believers are there in chapter twenty-one? Phrases such as *more than these* (v. 15) and *when you grow old* (v. 18) indicate that we are required to pay a price that Christ may have the opportunity to fill us richly with Himself.

Although in John 20 Peter had already been saved, inwardly he did not have much room for Christ. He had received the eternal life abundantly, but he had not been sufficiently filled with Christ. Therefore, the Lord said, "Do you love Me more than these?" (21:15). To have more love for the Lord would require him to pay a price. If we only have faith, we still cannot say that for us to live is Christ, we still cannot know the power of Christ's resurrection, and we still cannot say that it is God who operates in us both the willing and the working. The Lord said that anyone who does not forsake all that he has cannot be His disciple (Luke 14:26, 33). If merely having faith were enough, then Paul would not have needed to run the race (1 Cor. 9:24, 26; Gal. 2:2; 2 Tim. 4:7), nor would he have desired to receive the reward in the future (Phil. 3:14).

THE RESULT OF PAYING A PRICE

What is the result of paying a price? The result is that by handing yourself and all you have over to God, God and all that He has are mingled with you. Paying a price is not only for you to receive a reward and be raptured in the future. Rather, it is for you and all that you have to be taken away and for God and all that He has to be added to and mingled with you. Those who are raptured first are those who have been filled with God. Those who enter into the kingdom to receive a reward are those who have been filled with Christ. Those who participate in the out-resurrection are those who have lived in the power of Christ's resurrection today. Strictly speaking, it is not those who pay a price who will enter into the kingdom. Rather, it is only those who have paid a price and are thereby filled with Christ who will be able to enter into the kingdom. It is not the price itself that qualifies you to enter into the kingdom, nor is it the price itself that gives you the qualification to be a king. Rather, it is the Christ with whom you are filled who brings you into the kingdom and qualifies you to be a king.

If you want to be filled with Christ, you need to pay a price. God's element cannot come into you unless your element goes out. If you are short of God, you cannot mature early. If you are short of Christ, you will lose your qualification to be a king. Therefore, the result of paying a price is not that you will enter into the kingdom to receive a reward but that you will receive more of God and of Christ. However, those who are full of God and full of Christ are those who will ripen and be raptured first, and only such ones will enter into the kingdom and reign on the throne.

If all day long children think only about receiving their parents' possessions but do not love their parents, they are as unreasonable as robbers. If we do not pay a price, love God, or pursue the Lord, but all day long we only think about being raptured and receiving a reward, then we are just daydreaming. On the contrary, if children do not care for their parents' possessions but only know to constantly love their parents and to please them, eventually all that the parents have will be theirs. We should not consider the reward, the rapture, and the kingdom to be the goals of our pursuit. Madame Guyon said that we have become fallen if we pursue the reward merely for the reward itself. The goal of all our pursuits should be God and Christ, and we should pay any cost to gain Him. If we would pursue with such singleness of heart, how could we not mature early? How could we not receive the reward?

If you read the biography of George Müller, you will see that in every matter he sought God's leading and tried to sense God's feeling in fellowship. He wrote a book with the title, *Narrative of the Lord's Dealings with George Müller,* which corresponds exactly with the content of the book. He sought the Lord in fellowship regarding every matter, whether great or small, in his living. One thing which is deeply impressive is that after his death, people tried to make an inventory of his belongings, yet they found none, because he had completely handed over himself and all that he had for the sake of Christ. In man's eyes, he was so destitute after his death, unlike many people today who leave a great inheritance after their death for their children to fight over. However, in God's eyes, Müller was a person who was according to God's heart and who pleased God.

We have said again and again that the purpose of paying a price is for us to gain God and to have God added to and mingled with us, thereby replacing everything of ourselves. People who desire this willingly reject their natural life and disposition and take God's life and nature. They live and walk not by their own wisdom but by God's wisdom, and they forsake their possessions, relatives, fame, and position and want only God to come into them to be their all. This is what is meant in the Bible when it says that we must leave all and follow the Lord and suffer the loss of all things in order to gain Christ. This is what it means to pay the price, and this is the result of paying the price. Only people who pay the price have God operating in them both the willing and the working, have Christ being magnified in them all the time, whether through life or through death, and can say that for them to live is Christ. They are filled with Christ, filled with God, and can be used by God.

In summary, the first requirement for our being used by God is God's visitation, which is not of us but of God. God's visitation is His coming to us to visit with us. This is the beginning of God's using us. Whenever we have a desire to serve God, we know assuredly that God has reached us and visited us. However, merely having such a desire does not enable us to be used by God, because on our side we still have to pay a price.

One day God came to Isaiah, and as a result Isaiah was determined to go and work for God (Isa. 6:1-8). However, at that time he could not be used by God. He still had to pay a price. The result of paying a price is that by giving up all that we have, we take in all that God has. Only people like this can be used by God. Therefore, paying a price is the basic requirement and fact for us to be useful to God.

CHAPTER THREE

BEING USED BY THE LORD
AND THE OVERFLOW OF LIFE

WORKING FOR GOD BY THE OVERFLOW OF LIFE

Many children of God often consider that to work for the Lord is to be used by Him. It is true that to be used by the Lord is to work for Him, but what does it mean to work for Him? Today by the Lord's mercy we have clearly seen that working for the Lord is not a matter of how many things we accomplished for Him but of how much of the Lord's life overflows from us and is imparted through us. Brother Watchman Nee often said, "Genuine work is the overflow of life." Of course, our work contains an element of accomplishing certain things. However, we do not work for the sake of accomplishing things. Instead, we work that we may overflow the Lord's life, imparting and ministering the Lord's life to others, that is, imparting the Lord Himself to others.

Take preaching the gospel as an example. Our work for the Lord in this matter is to lead people to salvation on the one hand and to dispense the Lord's life into sinners on the other hand. With regard to the edification of the believers, on the one hand, we need to feed them, but on the other hand, our real intention is to dispense the Lord's life into them more and more. In our fellowship with the brothers and sisters or in our going out to visit the saints, apparently we are helping and establishing people. Actually, if our fellowship and visitations are up to the standard, there should be the overflow of the Lord's life and the dispensing of the Lord's life into the brothers and sisters. Even if we simply utter a few words of consolation and encouragement, there should be the overflowing of the Lord's life into the brothers and sisters. John

7:38 indicates that the Lord's intention is that we who have the Lord's life would flow out rivers of living water, the water of life, from within us to minister to the needs of many.

The reason the Catholic Church and the Protestant churches have become a great tree (Matt. 13:32) is that they have many accomplishments and enterprises but lack the life within. In the Catholic Church there are many works and undertakings, but there is hardly any of the element of life. It is the same with many of the Protestant denominations. They have enterprises such as evangelistic missions, schools, and hospitals. However, in all these large-scale works, it is difficult for people to receive any of the element of life. Many times it is the same even among us. Often our activities, services, and works do not have much of the element of life.

THE OVERFLOW OF LIFE DEPENDING NEITHER ON ELOQUENCE NOR ON GIFTS

A message released from the platform may be convincing and inspiring, but it may not necessarily impart Christ's life to people. An exposition of the Scriptures may be interesting and enjoyable to people, but it may not necessarily impart Christ's life to them. On the contrary, a certain brother may stand up in the meeting to give a little testimony. He may lack eloquence and fluency in speech, and it may seem that he is unable to touch people's emotions. Nevertheless, after his speaking, the listeners have the feeling that something unexplainable, something spiritual, has come into them. It is as if the Lord came into them to touch their deepest parts, although they were not conscious of it. This is the overflow of life into others.

Sometimes when a certain brother stands up in the meeting to speak, his voice is loud and clear, and his words flow smoothly. He is able to arrest the audience's attention and cause them all to nod their heads in appreciation. However, after he is finished speaking, there is nothing left. This kind of message is like music that does not inspire. It is merely sounding brass and a clanging cymbal (1 Cor. 13:1). After the sounding and clanging are over, there is nothing left, and those who have heard it have not received any life. Sometimes you may go to visit a certain person. While you are sitting before him, he may not say anything, yet you sense that something has entered into you and touched your feelings. If you live by the flesh, the sense he gives you may touch and condemn your flesh. If you love sins and the world, the sense he gives you may touch a particular sin or a particular aspect of the world and even condemn it. On the contrary, you may meet a certain person who speaks a lot, yet not one of his words enters into you and touches your feelings. It seems that everything he says is in vain and useless. The first person did not speak many words to exhort you, but just by a little contact with you, he touched your problem. Although the second person spoke many words and quoted many verses, they had no effect on you. The difference between the two lies in the fact that one is able to impart life to others even though his speaking may not be fluent, while the other is unable to overflow life, although his words are many. Therefore, we have to see that genuine work is the overflow and imparting of life.

It is usually more miserable to be hungry in spirit than to be hungry in the flesh. In some local churches people feel miserable in their spirit when they go to the meetings, whereas in other local churches people sense the presence of the Spirit when they go. This all hinges on whether there is the overflow of life. If we try to convince people merely with doctrines, it will be useless. People can comprehend spiritual things only when they touch life. Therefore, when we touch spiritual matters, the question is, are we touching something of doctrine or of life? One time someone asked a brother, "Can a saved person still be in darkness?" The brother replied, "Are you in the light today?" That person asked a question in the mind, yet the brother answered him in life to touch his inner feeling. Hence, even while we are conversing with others, there is a difference between being in doctrine and being in life.

PAYING A PRICE TO ALLOW GOD TO WORK IN US

One time someone said to me, "We cannot say that the five virgins in Matthew 25 are saved ones." I then asked him, "Are all saved ones wise? Are you wise?" (cf. vv. 1-13). We have to see that constant debating about doctrines is useless. We can solve people's problems only by touching them in life. Only by the overflow of life can we touch people's inner being, and once we touch them in this way, something spiritual will enter into them. Therefore, to be used by God is to work for Him, and to work for Him is to overflow God's life, to dispense God's life and God Himself, to others. However, before we can dispense God to others, we ourselves must first have God and have life.

We can never flow out what we do not have, what we have not experienced, or what we have not received. We can flow out only what we have first received into us. Therefore, a person who intends to work for God must first let God work in him. Only one who has allowed God to work in him will be able to work for God. This is because a person can experience God only when he allows God to work in him. When he does, God's life will enter into him through his experiences, and then he will be able to flow out into others the life of God he has received. For this reason, we need to pay a price. To allow God to work in us is to pay a price. One who is not willing to pay this price can only preach doctrines but cannot dispense life to others.

CHAPTER FOUR

THE NEED TO GROW AND MATURE IN LIFE AFTER RECEIVING SALVATION

THE TRADITIONAL CONCEPT CONCERNING GOD'S SALVATION

In today's Christianity, including both Catholicism and Protestantism, most people do not have an accurate concept concerning God's salvation, nor do they have a clear knowledge of the economy and arrangement of God in His salvation. There is a widely accepted concept in Christianity today that is seemingly based on the Scriptures but is actually derived primarily from human speculation. This concept did not exist at the beginning of the church. Rather, it was an idea formed later through human conjecture and then further developed into a doctrine. Now it has evolved into a traditional concept that is prevailing in Christianity.

What is this concept? People who have this concept believe that we all are sinful, but because God had compassion toward us, He sent His only begotten Son to be our Savior. This One died for us on the cross, bore up our sins, resurrected and ascended to heaven, and is now continually interceding for us before God as our great High Priest. According to this concept, if a person who feels that he is a sinner and deserves to suffer perdition repents and believes in the Lord—receiving Him as his Savior and calling on Him—his sins will be forgiven, he will be reconciled to God, and God will be gracious to him and bestow blessing upon him. As a result, this person will become a saved one. Since God has been so gracious to him, from that point on he should show his gratitude to God by conducting himself in a manner that will glorify the name of God. After this person dies, his soul will go to heaven to enjoy eternal blessing. This is the so-called orthodox belief in today's Christianity.

COMPARING THE TRADITIONAL CONCEPT
WITH THE BIBLE

Is this concept correct? We must compare it carefully with the truth in the Scriptures. When Martin Luther compared the Catholic doctrine on the sacrament of penance with the biblical truth concerning justification by faith (Rom. 1:17), he found out that the teaching of doing penance was a man-made tradition based on human opinions and was altogether erroneous. Today we should also discern the authenticity of the so-called orthodox beliefs taught in Christianity by comparing them with the truth revealed in the Bible.

If we would abandon human opinions with the traditional concepts, not holding on to our ideas and views but simply coming to the Word of God, then we would see that in Christianity the current concept of God's salvation definitely contains certain inaccuracies and deficiencies. To be inaccurate is to be incorrect and in disagreement with the truth revealed in the Scriptures whereas to be deficient is to not measure up to the biblical truth in its richness and transcendence.

THE EMPHASIS OF THE GOSPELS OF LUKE AND JOHN—
SALVATION BY FAITH

The Gospels do not consist of one book but four books, and each of the Gospels has a different emphasis. For example, from the beginning to the end, the Gospel of Luke covers the truth of the forgiveness of sins, the gospel of forgiveness (24:47). It shows us that in God's eyes we were prodigal sons who were far away from God the Father and that we were also lost sinners and lost sheep (15:1, 6-7, 11-32). Therefore, God sent His Son as our Savior to find us and bring us back. God accepted us, the prodigal sons, when we repented and came back to Him. Even if we were like the disreputable woman in chapter seven who had many sins (vv. 36-50), the corrupt tax collector in chapter nineteen (vv. 1-10), or the robber on the cross in chapter twenty-three (vv. 32, 40-43), when we repented and believed in the Lord, receiving Him as our Savior, our sins were forgiven. This is the truth of the forgiveness of sins shown in the Gospel of Luke. Because the Lord Jesus Christ accomplished redemption on the cross, whoever believes in Him will receive the forgiveness of sins freely, without having to pay any price. This is the emphasis of the Gospel of Luke.

John preached the gospel of life. At the outset, the Gospel of John shows us that the Lord was God, that in Him was life, and that He became flesh (1:1, 4, 14). The reason He came from the heavens to the earth was that He intended to impart life to the world (10:10b). He said that He was a grain of wheat, and as such, He could not release the life from within Him for men to receive unless He fell into the ground, died, and resurrected. Therefore, one day He went to the cross and died, and on the third day He resurrected. Now at any time and in any place if someone believes in His name and receives Him as the Savior, He will enter into him as the Spirit that he may receive the life of God. In this way a person can be regenerated and have the life of God (3:3, 5, 15-16; 20:31). This is the grace of life. We receive this grace of life altogether by faith, without having to pay any price. This is clearly seen in the Gospel of John. Therefore, Luke and John both show us that we can receive the gospel, whether it be the gospel of the forgiveness of sins or the gospel of life, simply by faith. There is no need to pay any price or to fulfill any requirement.

THE EMPHASIS OF
THE GOSPELS OF MATTHEW AND MARK—
PAYING A PRICE

However, the Gospels comprise not only Luke and John but also Matthew and Mark. If we read through the Gospels of Matthew and Mark, we will discover that it is not so easy to find passages about salvation by faith. These two Gospels tell us to leave all that we have, to deny ourselves (Matt. 16:24; Mark 8:34-35), to enter in through the narrow gate and walk on the constricted way (Matt. 7:13-14), and to pay a considerably great price to follow the Lord Jesus. Although in some instances these two Gospels also refer to faith, the faith they mention is not the faith for receiving salvation but for walking on the way of the Lord. This is not the faith for receiving life but for living a daily life. The faith for our salvation is the faith by which we receive forgiveness of sins and the life of God. This is the faith revealed in Luke and John. However, after we are saved and have received the life of God, we still need to walk on the Lord's way and live a heavenly life. To walk such a way and live such a life we need the kind of faith referred to in Matthew and Mark.

Aside from passages concerning this kind of faith, it is difficult to find passages in Matthew and Mark telling us that faith is for us to be saved and to receive the life of God. Instead, in the Gospels of Matthew and Mark we are solemnly told numerous times that we should forsake everything, deny ourselves, and take up the cross to follow the Lord. This shows us the word of God in its completeness with its overall significance.

PAYING A PRICE BEING NECESSARY AFTER BELIEVING

Faith alone is not enough for us to fully enjoy God's salvation in its richness and extensiveness. Hence, after believing, we still need to pay a price to follow the Lord that we may enjoy such a rich salvation. Believing in the Lord is for us to receive Him whereas following the Lord is for us to enjoy Him. By believing we receive forgiveness of sins and the life of God, and the Lord comes into us as the Spirit. By following the Lord after we have been saved, we enjoy the Lord, have His presence, and allow Him to be everything to us, including our life and power every day.

Let us use an illustration. When your friend gives you a nice gift, you need only to receive it, and then you will have it. From the day you receive it, it is yours. However, if after receiving it you simply put it aside and do not spend any time to enjoy it, then even though you have received it and now possess it, you have not enjoyed it at all. Similarly, we receive and possess God's salvation just by believing. Once we believe, our sins are forgiven and we receive the life of God. Once we believe in the Lord, He comes into us. Furthermore, God and all that God has becomes ours. After we believe, however, we still have to pay a price. We need to make an effort every day to enjoy what we have received, taking the Lord in by eating and drinking Him in our spirit day by day. In this way He can then become the element within us in reality. If we do not pay such a price and do not make such an effort, we cannot practically and fully enjoy the salvation we have received.

THE CONDITION OF GOD'S CHILDREN TODAY

Today many of the children of God—although they have truly been saved, have the Lord's life in them, and also have the Holy Spirit dwelling in them—have not enjoyed the Lord or the salvation of God. Although they come to the meetings, listen to messages, and occasionally pray and read the Word, in their living and in their walk they are themselves, while the Lord is the Lord. They and the Lord have not been mingled to become one. They have not allowed the Lord to practically come into their daily living. They do whatever they like to do and say whatever they like to say. They have simply forgotten about the Lord and have put Him aside.

Although they have the Lord, they do not enjoy Him. They are like misers who have much money and yet do not use their money. They are saved ones who have the Lord's life and the Lord's presence, yet they do not enjoy the Lord. They live by themselves according to the lusts of the flesh, following the tide of this world. They are just like unsaved people, living in the world in a common way. The only difference is that they confess that there is a God while the unsaved people do not. They believe in the Lord while the unsaved people do not. They believe in the eternal life while the unsaved people do not. In addition, sometimes when their hearts are touched by the grace of God, their hearts become filled with gratitude toward God whereas unsaved people do not have such experiences. Christians of this kind are different from unsaved people in their beliefs, but in their daily walk they are the same as the unsaved. Just as the unsaved ones love the world, live for the world, and struggle for fame and wealth, so also do these saved ones. Just as the unsaved ones live by themselves in their flesh and in their natural being, being neither under the rule of God nor under the authority of the kingdom, so also do the saved ones. They already have the life of God in them, yet they do not live by God's life. To them, God is no more than an object for them to believe in. This is the abnormal condition of many of God's children today.

THE EMPHASIS OF PAUL'S EPISTLES

However, the four Gospels show us that God's salvation is not like this. Luke and John show us from one side that upon believing in the Lord, we receive forgiveness of sins and the life of God. Matthew and Mark show us from another side that from the day we were saved, we who have been forgiven of our sins and have received the life of God should follow the Lord and take the Lord as our life and our living. We must live by the Lord's life. For this reason, we have to pay a price, leave everything we have, deny ourselves, and take up the cross to follow the Lord. This is the salvation of God seen in the four Gospels.

In the Epistles we see that the Galatians undoubtedly believed in the Lord. Their sins were forgiven, and they had the life of God, yet they lived by themselves, relying too much on themselves rather than on the life of Christ. The apostle Paul said to them, "My children, with whom I travail again in birth..." (Gal. 4:19). Why did he travail again in birth for them? Was it for them to be saved again? It was not. Was it for them to be forgiven of their sins again? It was not. Was it for them to receive the life of God again? It was not! Then what was it for? It was for Christ to be formed in them. To be saved is one thing, but to have Christ formed in us is another thing.

THE PURPOSE OF GOD'S SALVATION NOT BEING
TO SAVE US TO GO TO HEAVEN

The unique purpose of God's salvation is for God to come into us and mingle Himself with us. God wants to come into us to be our life (Col. 3:4a) and to grow in us (2:19b). Although the goal of our salvation includes the blessing of entering into the kingdom, it is not restricted merely to such a blessing. Rather, the ultimate goal of our salvation is for us, the saved ones, to be mingled with God that Christ may make His home in our hearts through faith (Eph. 3:17) as our life and that we may grow up unto maturity (4:13).

Unfortunately, due to erroneous teachings, there is the mistaken concept in traditional Christianity that a saved one, one who believes in the Lord and whose sins are forgiven, will go to heaven when he dies. According to this concept, if a believer has a heart that fears the Lord, and if in his daily life he reads the Bible, prays to the Lord, attends the meetings, helps others, and pleases the Lord, then the Lord will bestow many blessings on him. As a result, he will be able to glorify the Lord, and he himself will also have peace in his heart. According to the concept in Christianity, this is the greatest honor of being a Christian. This is the traditional religious concept, but it is not the goal of God's salvation. The goal of God's salvation is that the believers gradually grow and mature in life until, consummately, they are exactly the same as Christ.

How does God accomplish such a salvation? First, He sent His only begotten Son to die on the cross for our sins. Then in Christ and as the Spirit (1 Cor. 15:45b), He enters into us to live in us as our life. Christ is not only living in us (Gal. 2:20) but also growing in us. He intends to grow, to be formed, and to mature in us (Eph. 4:13). This is God's saving way. What does it mean to grow unto maturity? To grow unto maturity means that Christ lives in us as our life and that He continually grows in us to the extent that He is formed in us. When Christ is fully formed in us, we will be mature in His life.

If we read through the entire Bible, we are unable to find any statement saying that those who believe in Jesus will go to heaven after they die. Such a concept did not exist in the first two centuries. It was altogether a notion brought in by degraded Catholicism. Instead, the Bible tells us that after a person believes in the Lord, the Lord enters into him to be his life and to grow, be formed, and eventually mature in him. This is the salvation of God revealed in the Scriptures. This is much different from the traditional yet erroneous concept of going to heaven.

THE PARABLE OF THE HARVEST

The Bible also tells us that after a person has been saved and has received the Lord's life, he becomes part of the crop in the Lord's field (Rev. 14:15-16). Would the master reap the harvest and gather it into the barn before it is ripe? Of course he would not. Revelation 14 tells us that among the Christians a small number of overcomers will be raptured to the heavens before the harvest. They are the firstfruits, the produce that has ripened first.

In northern China by the month of April the wheat in the field has grown very tall and displays a golden color. This indicates that the wheat has ripened thoroughly. The owner of the field first goes and reaps the firstfruits and brings them home. Then at the Double Fifth Festival, the family eats the firstfruits for their special enjoyment. After another two weeks the rest of the harvest in the field ripens, and the owner reaps the crop and brings it into the barn. Matthew 13 clearly tells us that the field refers to the world, and the barn refers to the kingdom of the Father (vv. 24, 30, 38, 43). Today we are God's crop growing in the field—the world—until we become thoroughly ripened. Then God will come to reap us and bring us into the eternal barn.

If the crop were not ripe but still green and tender, the owner of the field would never harvest the crop and bring it into the barn. Likewise, there is no question that the saved ones will enter into the kingdom. However, there is a condition—they need to be ripe. The earth is the field, and the heavens are the barn. What is the requirement for us, the crop, to be gathered from the field on the earth into the barn in the heavens? The requirement is that we need to be ripe. Only the ripe ones can be gathered into the barn. The unripe ones will be left in the field to continue growing. As wheat grows, it enjoys the elements of the soil, the supply of water, and the provision of fertilizer. If the wheat could speak, it would say, "This is very sweet! What an enjoyment I have here!" However, when the crop is being ripened, it undergoes a great amount of suffering. Not only is the fertilizer withheld and the water reduced, but the wheat is also exposed to the intense heat of the sun to make it turn from being greenish to being golden. Likewise, when a person who belongs to the Lord is newly saved, he enjoys a very sweet period of time. However, unless he goes on to pay a price, be dealt with, and have the experience of being exposed to the sun, he cannot readily grow and become mature.

THE IMMATURE ONES NOT BEING ABLE TO ENTER INTO THE KINGDOM

The only kind of people who can enter into the kingdom are those who are mature. If we read through Revelation carefully, we can see that all the Christians who will be in the kingdom will be the ripened ones. Those who do not ripen cannot enter into the kingdom. This is similar to the fact that all the produce that is in the barn is ripe. The produce that is not yet ripe has to remain in the field until it is ripened either through the heat of the sun or the blowing of the wind. It must be ripened before it can be harvested. Likewise, although all Christians have been saved, they cannot enter into the kingdom without being matured. Therefore, the thought that the soul of a Christian goes to heaven after he dies is shallow and childish. It is not the truth revealed in the Bible but the tradition of Roman Catholicism. The notion of going to heaven is not in the Bible.

HEAVENLY MANSION BEING A RELIGIOUS TERM

The term *heavenly mansion* is not found in the Bible. Rather, it is an expression that is used in religion. The Bible only uses the words *heaven* and *heavens*. In the Chinese translation of the Bible the translators borrowed the term *heavenly mansion* and used it because it had been widely adopted by religion at the time they were doing their translation. In the Chinese Union Version the term *heavenly mansion* is found in two places—in 1 Peter 3:22 and also in Hebrews 9:24. However, in the original text the word *heaven* is used in both places. It was to heaven that the Lord ascended after His death and resurrection (Mark 16:19; Luke 24:51; Acts 1:11). In the Bible there is no thought of "going to a heavenly mansion," and there is no verse telling us that the souls of Christians go to a heavenly mansion after they die. When a believer dies, his spirit and soul do not go to heaven but to Paradise in Hades (Luke 23:43).

It is correct to say that Christians will one day enter into the kingdom, but they must first be mature before they can do so. Perhaps someone may wonder, "Many of the brothers and sisters have truly received forgiveness of sins and the Lord's life. However, since the time they were saved, they have not paid a price, lived an overcoming life, or faithfully followed the Lord. It is obvious that they do not have the maturity in life. What will their future be?" There was once a certain brother who was truly saved. However, after he was saved, he still loved the world, lived by his flesh, loved money, and did not love God. One day he died of a stroke after falling into a terrible rage. Then the brothers and sisters gathered together to sing some hymns on his behalf and to speak a word of consolation, saying, "Thank and praise the Lord that our brother has gone to heaven, to the heavenly home. He is really blessed!" Where can you find such a teaching in the holy Scriptures? The Bible says that it is not until the harvest is ripe that the crop will be reaped and brought into the eternal barn. In the Scriptures the destiny of the believers is decided according to maturity. Those who mature earlier will be gathered into the barn earlier while those who mature later will be brought into the barn later. This is clearly revealed in the Bible.

Then where did that brother go after his death if he did not go to heaven? This is not hard to understand. Do you remember the robber who repented on the cross? He said to the Lord, "Jesus, remember me when You come into Your kingdom." The Lord replied immediately, "Today you shall be with Me in Paradise" (Luke 23:42-43). Furthermore, Matthew 12 and Acts 2 both tell us that after His death, the Lord was in Hades three days and three nights (Matt. 12:40; Acts 2:24-27). By studying these verses carefully, we can readily understand that Paradise is in Hades. This is also referred to in Luke 16. Abraham's bosom—the place where Lazarus was, across from the place where the rich man was—was the Paradise in Hades (vv. 23-24).

PARADISE NOT HAVING BEEN TRANSFERRED
FROM HADES TO HEAVEN

Most theologians in Christianity also acknowledge this fact. However, some believe that before the resurrection of the Lord Jesus, this Paradise was indeed in Hades and that after the Lord's resurrection, Paradise was moved by the Lord from Hades to heaven. They say this based upon Ephesians 4:8, which says, "Having ascended to the height, He led captive those taken captive." They quote this verse as the basis of the transfer of Paradise. However, the phrase *He led captive those taken captive* means that prior to the Lord's resurrection, when men died they were taken captive to Hades by the power of death—the power of Satan. Then at the time of His resurrection, the Lord Jesus overcame the devil, who has the might of death, and broke through Hades, thereby leading captive those taken captive. Therefore, this verse does not mean that Hades was moved to heaven.

After the believers die, their spirits go to Hades, while their bodies are buried in graves. For example, after Peter and Paul died, their bodies were buried in the earth, but their spirits were disembodied. Disembodied spirits are abnormal because they still bear the sign of death. Although Peter and Paul were saved ones, death was still in them and had not been removed. At the Lord's return their spirits will come out of Hades and their bodies will also come out of the graves to become glorious bodies. At that time their bodies and spirits will be joined together. When their spirits are clothed with their bodies again, then they will be able to enter into the presence of God. In the Bible disembodied spirits are naked spirits, which still bear the sign of death and therefore cannot enter into the presence of God. It is not until the time of rapture, when the spirits of the saved ones will come out of Hades and will put on their transfigured bodies, being fully dressed with proper attire, that they will be able to go to God.

THE IMMATURE ONES STILL NEEDING TO DEAL
WITH THE MATTER OF MATURITY
AFTER BEING RESURRECTED

The believers who die without being matured in life will be

unable to go into the presence of God even after being clothed in resurrection. In Matthew 25 we are told that at the time of resurrection the saints who are ready and mature will attend the Lord's wedding feast while the immature ones will still have to pay a price to reach maturity. In other words, if as a Christian you die without reaching maturity, then at the time of resurrection you will still have to complete the process of maturing. Do not expect to go to the Lord without completing the process of maturing.

Hence, whoever wants to attend the Lord's wedding feast will have to be matured. There is only one kind of Christian in the heavens—Christians who are mature. If you have become mature in your lifetime, you are already prepared, and you can praise the Lord for this. Like the five prudent virgins, you can go in to the Lord's wedding feast at His coming. However, if you have not prepared yourself and have not become mature in your lifetime, then if unfortunately you die, after your resurrection you will still have to deal with the issue of maturity. After you are resurrected, like the five foolish virgins, you will still need to pay the price to buy the oil.

Therefore, as Christians we must be matured. This is the goal we all must attain to. The Lord's intention to mature in us is a matter that we cannot avoid. If we do not walk on this way and do not arrive at this goal, then we should not expect to one day go in to the Lord's wedding feast. If you do not pay the price to arrive at maturity yet expect to enter into the kingdom, then one day your expectation will be proven to have been in vain.

We became Christians upon believing in the Lord, but has Christ become full-grown in us? We have been saved and have Christ's life in us, but has this life become mature? We must remember that this life has to mature either now or in the future. If we settle this question of maturity while we are still alive today, we are the prudent virgins. If we are not matured, then at the time of resurrection we will still have to resolve this matter of maturity, because the Bible tells us that after we are saved, we need to grow unto maturity in life. This is God's salvation.

CHAPTER FIVE

THE ECONOMY OF GOD'S GRACE

Many Christians do not have a clear, accurate knowledge of the truth concerning the plan of God's salvation and the economy of God's grace. The terms *economy,* or *plan,* and *stewardship* were used by Paul in Ephesians 1:10 and 3:2, 9. Unfortunately, they are not properly translated in the Chinese Union Version.

GOD BEING A GOD WITH A PLAN AND AN ECONOMY

Ephesians 1:10 says, "Unto the economy of the fullness of the times." The Greek word for *economy* also means "dispensation," "plan," or "management." Just as a businessman knows how to manage his wealth, so also God has His management, His economy, in the universe. However, what God manages in His economy in the universe is His grace.

We have already seen that God has a plan for saving us and an economy for dispensing grace to us. Just as a businessman has a plan for the management of his business, so the great God has His plan for distributing grace among the human race. Ephesians chapters one and three speak about the plan, the economy, of God's mystery. If we read the book of Ephesians carefully, we will see that it is quite complicated and not as simple as we think.

In many people's concepts salvation means merely that God loved us and sent His Son to accomplish redemption for our sins, so that as long as we believe in Him, our sins will be forgiven and we will go to heaven to enjoy eternal blessings. If this is indeed the salvation of the God whom we serve, then it is admittedly too simple. If we study the entire Bible in a detailed way, we will see that God's salvation is not so simple.

Therefore, we need to meditate on the Word of God carefully that we may enter deeply into the thought of the Scriptures.

In reading the Word we must not take any chapter or any verse out of context. We cannot grasp one or two sentences in the Bible and then assert that God's salvation is such and such. To do so would be very dangerous. If we would meditate on the New Testament as a whole, we would realize that the common concept in Christianity is much different from God's revelation through the holy Scriptures. Today the Lord has opened the truths to the churches in His recovery, so we should not hide them. Nevertheless, we also do not want these truths to become material for argument. If this happens, not only would it deprive people of the supply of life, but it will also become a hindrance to them. Whatever we do must be for others to get help and be established.

THE MISTAKE OF CATHOLICISM

In order to adjust the inaccurate concepts of the past, we must first point out what they are. Catholicism and Protestantism have done much to harm people's spiritual lives, the Lord's work, and God's economy. The reason many have been damaged by Catholicism and Protestantism is that they do not have an accurate, thorough knowledge of the truth. One example is the matter of purgatory. Catholicism teaches that after a person dies, he has to be disciplined in purgatory for the sins he committed in the past. Therefore, before he dies, he should try his best to do penance, and even after his death his relatives can also do penance on his behalf so that he can be raised out of purgatory. This is a damaging doctrine taught in Catholicism.

Many in Catholicism have the thought that while a person is alive, he does not need to apply the effectiveness of the Lord's precious blood. If he sins, he only has to confess his sin to the Catholic priests to be forgiven. While a person is alive, he does not need to fear God or live a holy life to please God, because before he dies, he can simply give some money and do some good deeds for the atonement of his sins. Even if he himself cannot do this, his family members can make up for him by holding Mass on his behalf to raise his soul out of the sufferings of purgatory. It is surprising that such a thought, such a concept, can exist in Catholicism and that it is believed and accepted by almost all Catholics. If you tell them that this is heresy, they would say that it is ordained by the pope. If you say that this is not scriptural, they would say that it was decreed by the pope. In the eyes of many Catholics, they only have the pope.

THE MISTAKE OF PROTESTANTISM

Revelation 12 tells us about the man-child who, because he overcame, was caught up to God and to His throne before the great tribulation of three and a half years (v. 5). Then in chapter fourteen we see the hundred and forty-four thousand who, because they followed the Lamb, were raptured to Mount Zion in the heavens while the Antichrist was acting lawlessly on the earth (vv. 1-5). The words in the holy Scriptures are so clear that they allow no room for human doubt. Furthermore, 1 Thessalonians 4 tells us also that when the Lord descends from heaven, the dead believers who will be resurrected and the living believers who will be transfigured will be brought together to meet Him in the air (vv. 15-17).

While the Lord Jesus was on the cross, the repentant robber asked a favor of Him, saying, "Jesus, remember me when You come into Your kingdom" (Luke 23:42). If the Lord had answered the robber according to his request, He would have had to wait for a long, long time—the time that would pass before He came into His kingdom—before He could remember the robber. Yet He answered, "Today you shall be with Me in Paradise" (v. 43). Where is the Paradise mentioned by the Lord? Is it in heaven? It is not, because we know that the Lord went to Hades as soon as He expired. This was the fulfillment of what He had said concerning the Son of Man being in the heart of the earth three days and three nights (Matt. 12:40). From this we can see that the Paradise which the Lord mentioned to the robber is in Hades. The Lord's speaking is clear and accurate, and it leaves no room for doubt and conjecture. Hence, we must examine this matter according to the revelation of the Bible, rather than follow the mistaken concept of "going to heaven" generally accepted in Protestantism.

THE THOUGHT IN THE HOLY SCRIPTURES

The Bible never says that the soul of a person who has believed in Jesus and has been saved will go to a heavenly mansion when he dies. It is true that the Chinese Union Version has the term *heavenly mansion,* but this is because of the way this word was translated. The Greek word should be properly translated as *heavens.* This is the same word as the word that is translated *heavens* in the phrase *the kingdom of the heavens has drawn near* (Matt. 3:2; 4:17; 10:7). According to the biblical record, *heavens* refers to the third heaven, the habitation of God. In the Chinese Union Version, this word was translated as *heavenly mansion* in only two places in the entire New Testament—Hebrews 9:24 and 1 Peter 3:22. *Heavenly mansion* is a term used in Chinese Buddhism to refer to nirvana, a place of perfect bliss. However, *heavens* in these two portions of the Word refers to the third heaven where God dwells.

The Bible tells us that at the final age, at the coming of the new heavens and the new earth, the holy city New Jerusalem, the habitation of God, will come down out of heaven from God (Rev. 21:2, 10). At that time all the saved ones will undoubtedly be there enjoying eternal blessings with God. Not only their souls will be there, but their entire being—spirit, soul, and body—will also be filled with the divine element, and they will be in the habitation of the God of glory, mingled with Him and living with Him eternally.

I hope we all can see that God's salvation comes out of His plan and that God's giving of grace to us comes out of His economy. Some English versions of the Bible use the word *economy* or *dispensation,* which means "arrangement" or "distribution." These expressions show that God's giving of grace involves His economy, administration, and dispensation. The Bible says that the God who works all things dispenses grace to us according to the eternal purpose which He made in Christ (Eph. 1:11; 3:8-11). This God who has an expectation, a purpose, a plan, and an economy, does not give grace to us according to His whim. Rather, His giving of grace is His distribution of grace according to His economy, His dispensation.

GOD'S THOUGHT CONCERNING SALVATION— THAT WE MAY BE CONFORMED TO THE IMAGE OF GOD'S SON

If we carefully read through the Bible, we can find God's thought concerning salvation. Every person who manages a business has a thought concerning his management, and the administration and arrangement of his business is based upon this thought. Likewise, God also has a thought concerning the economy and dispensation of giving grace to us. Today in Christianity the prevailing concept is that we were once sinful but that after we believed in the Lord and received God's forgiveness, we were saved. Thus, after we die, our souls will go to heaven to enjoy eternal blessings. Remember, however, that this is man's concept, not God's concept.

Romans 8:29 says that "those whom He [God] foreknew, He also predestinated." For what did God predestinate them? Was it for them to go to heaven? It was not. Verse 30 goes on to say, "And those whom He predestinated, these He also called." Did He call them so that they could go to heaven? No, He did not. The verse continues, "And those whom He called, these He also justified." Did He justify them so that they could go to heaven? No, He did not. The Word says that these "He also predestinated to be conformed to the image of His Son." God saves us not for us to go to heaven but for us to be conformed to the image of His Son.

Ephesians 1 says that God "chose us in Him [Christ] before the foundation of the world...unto sonship through Jesus Christ" (vv. 4-5). God's intention is that we become sons of God. Then chapter four says that His desire is that we, the saved ones, arrive at a full-grown man, at the measure of the stature of the fullness of Christ (v. 13). First John 3 says that undoubtedly "now we are children of God," yet "it has not yet been manifested what we will be." John also says that, nevertheless, at the Lord's return "we will be like Him." Furthermore, he says, "Everyone who has this hope set on Him purifies himself, even as He is pure" (vv. 2-3).

In view of this, what is God's thought? God's thought is not as simplistic as our thought. The Bible tells us that God has a pleasure in His heart, and according to His pleasure, He intends to gain a group of people to be vessels of His glory in the future. Like a potter, God made us with clay. We were just lumps of clay, yet we were created by God to be vessels, even vessels that He had prepared beforehand unto glory. God's intention is to put Himself as glory into us that we may become vessels of glory (Rom. 9:20-24). What grace this is! Just as a glass can contain grape juice, so we also can contain God. However, because the glass is a dead vessel, the grape juice cannot change the glass or be mingled with the glass. However, as living vessels of God, we contain the living God with the living Spirit and life. Thus, we can be mingled with God.

Thank God that on the day we were saved, God came into us, and as soon as He entered into us, a fellowship was brought in between Him and us, us and Him (1 John 1:3). Once fellowship is brought in, transformation begins (2 Cor. 3:18). I believe that we all have this kind of experience. At the time we were saved, God came into us, and from then on, He has been interfering with everything in our daily life—our speaking, our doing, our intentions, our thoughts, and our motives. This One who is in us is living. As He lives in us, He bothers us and fellowships with us all the time, producing an effect within us. The more intense this effect is, the more we are transformed inwardly.

This transformation takes place first in our spirit and then gradually reaches our mind (Rom. 12:2; Eph. 4:23). When this happens, our mind has the element of God. Gradually this transformation reaches our emotion, and as a result, we can no longer be as free as we were before in expressing our joy, anger, sorrow, and delight. We can no longer be free to love what we want to love. When we want to love someone or something with our love, the One in us holds us back and does not let us love. Formerly we loved as we pleased and lost our temper as we desired, but now it is not so convenient for us to do these things anymore. When we are about to love someone or to lose our temper, the One who is in us holds us back and bothers us, causing us to have no peace. Formerly, our ideas, decisions, choices, and preferences were all of ourselves. However, after God is mingled with us, everything is different and we are no longer so free. This is because God's element has been added into us.

In the past, once we had a certain idea or a definite opinion, no one could change us. Now it is different. When we are about to express our idea, He tugs on us from within. When we have a definite opinion, He mingles Himself with us. As we are praying, in our inner feeling we ask, "Does God want me to do this? Will He be happy if I do this?" In this way we have God's element and God's flavor in our ideas because God has been mingled with us. This mingling is conformation. The more mingling we have, the more we have the image of God's Son. Many brothers and sisters among us have some amount of the flavor of God's Son in their experience. This is because God is continually mingling Himself with them to conform them to the image of His Son.

The more God mingles Himself with us, the more we have His element. The more God mingles Himself with us, the more Christ spreads in us. Thus, Christ will gradually grow in us until He is formed and matured in us. Christ's being formed and matured in us causes us to become full-grown (Eph. 4:13). When we reach the stage of a full-grown man, Christ will be fully expressed through us. Christ will spread from our spirit to fully occupy our soul, and then He will permeate our body, and glory will be expressed. At that time, we will be matured and ready to be raptured because Christ will have fully grown and been fully formed in us.

First John 3:2 says, "If He is manifested, we will be like Him." Are we like Him now? How much is Christ expressed through us? Since the time we were saved, has there been more mingling of God in us? Whenever God moves in us, are we touched but not moved? Do we let Him prevail? Is God's element in our opinions and preferences? Perhaps to this day some among us may still have the concept that it is sufficient to be saved and "go to heaven" and that it is not necessary to be concerned about the matter of overcoming. Even some have said, "We do not expect to receive a reward. We are satisfied to serve as guards at the gates of the heavenly mansions." Furthermore, they say, "All the messages concerning the truth are very good, but we cannot measure up to them. They

are too difficult, so let us forget about them. Our God is a God
of compassion. He predestinated us not to be judged but to be
saved. Therefore, it is all right just to be saved. We should try
not to commit big sins, but if once in a while we commit small
sins, we don't have to think too much about it. We believers
should not be over zealous. Why should we go to meetings and
pray every day? It is enough just to be saved." However, if one
day such a one became seriously ill and was about to die, he
would not say this anymore. Instead, he would regret his
former attitude about grace. He would say to the Lord, "Lord,
You have saved me, and I truly know that You have forgiven
me of my sins and have given me the eternal life, so I do not
have any worries if You would take me today to be with You.
However, when I consider that in my whole life I have been
walking according to the flesh and caring only for myself,
when I consider that I have never thought about Your inter-
ests nor ever lived a single day for the gospel, how can I go to
see You peacefully? O Lord, have pity on me! If You would give
me a few more years, I would live them wholly for You." If he
would expire before finishing his words, would he then go to a
"heavenly mansion"? If he were to, would he not feel ashamed
when he saw the Lord at that "heavenly mansion"? A person
cannot go in a casual manner even to meet the president of a
nation, not to mention going to meet the Lord. At the very
least, he has to comb his hair, clean his face, and change his
clothes. Many people have been saved, but afterward they still
live by their flesh and natural life, love the world, indulge in
lusts, practice deceit, and do evil things, yet they still believe
that when they die, their souls will immediately go to a heavenly mansion. If this were the case, what kind of a place
would that heavenly mansion be? Would it not be a robbers'
den?

This is not God's thought concerning salvation. God's
intention is that all the saved ones would be conformed to the
image of His Son. Now consider yourself. Are your thoughts
filthy? Have they been purified by the Holy Spirit? Is your
natural being strong? Has it been dealt with by the Holy
Spirit? It is true that the Lord has bought and redeemed you
by His precious blood. Nevertheless, God will ask you how

much you have been transformed in His life. Have you been conformed to the image of His Son? Do you look like Him? God's salvation is not according to the doctrine taught in degraded Christianity but according to His purpose of grace. I am not asking whether you have been saved. I know that you already have been washed by the precious blood and that you also have received God's life, but do you live in Him? Are you under the ruling of the Spirit? Do you subject yourself to the heavenly authority? Are you being dealt with by the heavens?

ALL THINGS BEING IMPOSSIBLE WITH MEN BUT POSSIBLE WITH GOD

I know some will say, "I absolutely cannot make it." However, as long as you have the heart, the strength of God will come to you. "With men it is impossible, but not with God, for all things are possible with God" (Mark 10:27). He is our strength. The question is not whether we are able but whether we are willing. Are we willing to hate the world? Are we willing to hate the flesh? Are we willing to hate our natural being? It is regrettable that there are many who are simply not willing. They still continue to walk according to their flesh and still indulge in their lusts. I hope that we all would ask ourselves according to our conscience and our feeling, "Since we walk according to the flesh, indulge in lusts, and live altogether for ourselves, if we were to die today, would our souls immediately go to a 'heavenly mansion'?" There is no such logic even on earth, not to mention in the heavens. How can the harvest be gathered to the barn before it has ripened? The harvest must be ripened. The saved ones must grow unto maturity, and then they can be raptured and brought to God.

God has His economy, His administration, and His dispensation. God's salvation is not what many people imagine it to be—a matter of heaven and hell, of going to either heaven or hell. God has His plan, His arrangement, and in His grace He has His economy.

May the Lord have mercy on us that we may not be those who are disapproved (2 Cor. 13:6). We all should pray for the church and for the Lord to give grace to His church so that the church may go on in the way of His recovery. It has been more than four hundred years since the Reformation at the time of Martin Luther, and God is still recovering His truths. May we who live in these last days not allow the traditional errors to hinder the way of God's recovery. We all have the responsibility to carry out this commission.

CHAPTER SIX

HOW TO BE USEFUL IN THE LORD'S HAND

THE LIFE IN CHRISTIANS BEING A SERVING LIFE

One who serves God often asks, "How can I become one who is useful to the Lord? How can I become one who is useful in the Lord's hand, one who truly serves the Lord?" First, we must see that the Lord's life in us is a serving life. To see this characteristic requires revelation. Many Christians probably know that the Lord's life is holy, good, meek, bright, and so forth, but they do not know that the Lord's life in them is a serving life. Why is it that they do not know this? It is because their spiritual knowledge is often limited by their natural concept. In our natural concept we may have thoughts only concerning holiness, goodness, and meekness. We seldom have any thoughts about how to serve God. Actually, God's life comes into us that we may serve God.

ALL THE CHARACTERISTICS INHERENT IN THE LORD'S LIFE BEING FOR SERVICE

Revelation 21 and 22 show us that, on the one hand, the entire situation of the New Jerusalem is holy and bright (21:11, 18, 21, 23-25) and that, on the other hand, in the New Jerusalem, the final destination, there is eternal service to God (22:3-5). This clearly indicates that all those who are in the New Jerusalem are holy so that they may serve God. They are full of light so that they may serve God. They are good so that they may serve God. The life of the new creation, which they possess, is for them to serve God. All the characteristics inherent in the Lord's life, which is in us, are for service. Love is for service, light is for service, holiness is for service, righteousness is for service, goodness is for service, and spirituality is for service. All the special qualities inherent in the Lord's life are for service.

We may say that service is the goal while the special qualities inherent in the Lord's life are the qualifications and requirements for attaining to the goal—service. A life that is not holy cannot serve God. A life that is not bright cannot serve God. A life that is not righteous cannot serve God. A life that is not spiritual cannot serve God. The characteristics of life are not the goal. They are for us to attain to the unique goal—service to God.

THE LIFE IN THE GOSPELS

Many Christians long to be holy, spiritual, and victorious. However, we must ask why we long for these things. Why do we aspire to be holy? Why do we aspire to be spiritual? Why do we aspire to overcome? We should aspire to these things for only one purpose—serving God. The life in the Gospels is a life that is holy, bright, good, spiritual, heavenly, strong, and victorious. We must remember, however, that the purpose of such a life is service. The Lord Jesus' being holy was for service, His being righteous was for service, and His being strong and overcoming was for service. The Gospels show us that the life in Jesus the Nazarene was a serving life.

THE LIFE IN THE EPISTLES

Romans is a book that gives us the outline of God's salvation, the outline of the spiritual experience of a Christian, and the outline of the spiritual life of a Christian. In the beginning Romans shows us how we are saved and how we can have the Lord's life. Then it shows us how we should pursue holiness and victory. After having the experiences of sanctification and victory, chapter twelve tells us that we should offer our bodies as a living sacrifice, holy, well pleasing to God, and that this kind of service is reasonable (v. 1). This means that in our consecration we should experience a crisis, in which we leave the realm of not serving God and enter into the realm of serving God. However, many people do not see this matter. They do not realize that life is for service, salvation is for service, sanctification is for service, and over-coming is for service. All of our spiritual virtues are for service. Furthermore, service is not merely an outward behavior. Instead, service is the growth of the life in us. At the opening of Romans 12 Paul exhorted us to pass through the crisis of consecration, turning from the realm of not serving God to the realm of serving God. It seems that service is an outward act according to verse 1, but actually service is a story of the life that is within us. I believe we all have this kind of experience. As we kneel down to pray, giving ourselves to the Lord to love Him a little more, to draw near to Him a little more, and to allow His life to have a little more ground in us, immediately we have a desire to serve God. Within us is something inexplicable that urges us to serve God, to preach the gospel, to help the brothers and sisters, and to serve in the church. If we do not serve, we feel uncomfortable and uneasy, as if something is missing. If we serve, we feel comfortable, relaxed, at ease, and joyful. What does this mean? This means that the life within us is a serving life.

Many times we hear people praising, "O Lord, praise You that Your life is holy, powerful, bright, and spiritual." However, we seldom hear people saying, "O Lord, praise You that Your life is a serving life." Very few of us have seen that the Christian life is a ministering life, a life of service to God. We need to pray that the Lord would give us this light and this revelation, because it is a great and important revelation in the New Testament. The life in the Gospels is for service, and the life in Romans is also for service. The same is also true in the books of Corinthians and Ephesians. In Ephesians chapter four Paul tells us that as this life grows unto maturity, "all the Body, being joined together and being knit together through every joint of the rich supply and through the operation in the measure of each one part, causes the growth of the Body unto the building up of itself in love" (v. 16). What is this? This is ministry, and this is service.

THE LIFE IN REVELATION

At the end of the New Testament, when life has reached full growth and maturity, there is the New Jerusalem. What is the final issue of the New Jerusalem? Revelation 22:3-5 says that those who are in the New Jerusalem serve God forever and ever. In chapters twenty-one and twenty-two we see the manifestation of the New Jerusalem in the new heavens and new earth in eternity future. The New Jerusalem is the ultimate issue of God's work both in the old creation and the new creation throughout the ages, that is, both in God's work of creation and redemption. From the beginning of chapter twenty-one through verse 2 of chapter twenty-two we see the nature of the New Jerusalem. Then there are three short verses, verses 3 through 5, which show us what the people in the New Jerusalem will be doing. They will do nothing but serve God eternally.

THE FUNCTIONS FOR SERVICE
BEING THE OUTGROWTH OF THE LIFE WITHIN

On the day we were saved, the life of Christ entered into us. If we would love the Lord more and more, consecrate ourselves to Him, abandon our future, allow our natural life to be broken and our disposition to be dealt with, follow the spiritual light, and live in Christ, then the life within us will have the opportunity to grow from within. That outgrowth of life is our function, our service. Eventually, the function of a prophet grows out of one saint while the function of a teacher grows out of another. Out of a third saint grows the function of an elder while the function of a deacon grows out of another one, and the function of one who shows mercy grows out of still another one. All kinds of Christian functions grow out of the life within.

The functions for service to the Lord are not learned through seminaries. Instead, they are outgrowths of the life within. A person who serves the Lord is not necessarily a person with a degree. However, a person who serves the Lord is certainly a member of the Body. The function of any member is dependent upon the growth and strength of the life within that member. How does a child grow to be an adult? His growth does not require our teaching. It requires only that we provide him with different kinds of food that he may eat adequately and fulfill the requirements for the growth in life. Then one day he will naturally grow to be an adult.

Many people think that only those who are very wise can be used by the Lord and that since they themselves are foolish, they could never be used by the Lord. This is not true. Do not say, "I do not have eloquence, I do not know how to speak, and I cannot preach the word, so what am I good for? Only those who have a high level of eloquence, who can talk fluently and endlessly, are really good for something. Only they can really be used by the Lord." This is not true. Whether or not we are useful to the Lord depends solely on whether or not the Lord's life has had the opportunity to grow in us. We should ask ourselves, "Do I love the Lord? Have I consecrated myself to the Lord? Do I give the Lord's life the opportunity to grow? Do I allow the Lord's life to have a place in me? Have I cast aside my future? Am I willing to let my natural life and my flesh be broken and dealt with, allowing myself to be put aside?" Whether or not we are useful in the Lord's hand is not a question of whether or not we have the ability and capability to be useful but a matter of whether or not the life in us has grown.

SERVING THE LORD BY RELYING ON
THE INNER SOURCE OF LIFE

This one thing is true: the extent to which a person gives place to the Lord's life is the extent of his usefulness in the Lord's hand. Let me share a little testimony. What I am now is altogether different from what I was when I was a boy. In my childhood I was timid and secluded. I did not like to be with others but preferred to sit by myself, always avoiding others. In school I spoke very little with others. I did not enjoy participating in activities, and I had nearly no contact with others. At home when guests came, I would find an opportunity to slip away because whenever I saw people, I would blush and my lips would tremble when I spoke. That was the natural me. One day, however, the Lord called me to rise up and speak for Him, and from that day on I consecrated myself daily, received dealings daily, and learned to live in the Lord daily. In 1947 while I was in Shanghai, I met a brother who said to me, "Brother Lee, when you were young, you must have been a very popular student and a skillful speaker." I replied, "Brother, you are wrong. If you were to go and ask my schoolmates, you would find out that I am altogether different from what I was when I was young. It is like there are two different persons."

Regardless of what you are in your natural man, when you are willing to give place to the life of Christ, then He will live out of you. He will change your being and make you different, even absolutely different, from what you were before. Formerly you disliked activities, but now He wants you to be active. You may have disliked quietness, but now He wants you to be quiet. You may not have liked to speak, but now He wants you to speak. You may not have liked to contact people, but now He wants you to contact people. He will change you thoroughly.

In the early days nearly every time I stood up to speak for the Lord, I had stomach problems, and the pain was indescribable. All I could do was pray and consecrate myself, and then the next time I spoke, I would have to pray and consecrate again. It was by being desperate that in the Lord's hand I was able to break through. This is where our usefulness is. Usefulness is not something we have naturally nor something we have by birth. Rather, it is only when Christ finds a way, an opportunity, and an outlet to come out of us that we will be useful.

An elderly sister often says to me, "Brother Lee, it seems that you can never finish speaking. After you speak, you have more to speak." Actually, the fact that I can be here is altogether because of the Lord's mercy and grace. I have so many things to speak about because within me there is a source— the boundless source of the eternal life. The only question is whether or not we will limit Him. If we limit Him, we are finished, and we have nothing. What we have learned in our mind is very limited, but the source of life within us is unlimited.

I can testify to you that many times what I spoke on the platform was something that I had not considered even half an hour before the meeting. I have found a secret in speaking. The secret is that every time I am going to speak, I must have a strong consecration. I pray, "O Lord, here is a person who perhaps has been a little loose at other times, but at this time he wants to absolutely place himself in Your hands, absolutely put himself aside, and absolutely forget himself. Lord, may You come forth. May You work and come out of this person." Sometimes I would do this half an hour before the meeting, but at other times it was not until after the singing of the first hymn that someone would come to tell me, "Brother Lee, please speak." At such a time what could I say? I had to immediately put on the girdle—not the outward girdle but the inward girdle—and say to the Lord, "Lord, I am in Your hands. Please come forth." It was in this way that the words began to flow out and the message was released.

Therefore, we serve the Lord not by relying on ourselves but by depending on the One who is within us. Our capital and our resources are not the natural things we possess. Rather, our capital and our resources are the life within us, which is the living Christ, the boundless Christ. The problem is that although we have such a Christ, we do not give Him any ground. We have such a life, yet we do not give this life any opportunity to grow. We do not consecrate ourselves absolutely to the Lord, and we have not been dealt with and broken thoroughly. Because we do not allow Him to have the ground and the opportunity to grow, He cannot come out, and therefore we cannot minister to people. All our service hinges on His life. What we minister is His life, and the strength to minister is also His life. Once He has gained a place in us, we will become useful, and we will be able to minister, to serve. How wonderful this is!

LIFE MANIFESTING DIFFERENT FUNCTIONS FOR DIFFERENT SERVICES

The life and the blood cells that flow to the ears to enable us to hear also flow to the eyes to enable us to see, flow to the mouth to enable us to speak, and flow to the legs to enable us to walk. The life is the same, and the blood cells are also the same, but they manifest different functions in different members. We all have exactly the same life in us—the life of Christ. When this life gains a place in you, it may manifest the function of a teacher. When it gains a place in someone else, it may manifest the function of an elder. When it gains a place in me, it may manifest the function of a deacon. Although the functions manifested are different, the life is still one, and Christ is still one.

The difference is not in nature but in function, and the different functions are for different services. Service comes out of this and is based upon this. When the life of Christ gains a place in us, it will manifest a function. This is ministry, and this is service.

FIVE MATTERS FOR OUR EXERCISE

Question: Why is it that with many Christians their function before the Lord is not manifested?

Answer: Let us consider what our use is before the Lord. We may be very zealous, willing to pursue the Lord, and regular in attending the meetings, but what is our use in the Lord's hands? I believe everyone would probably say that he does not know. In the local churches everywhere, we can see that there are many brothers and sisters who are zealous for the Lord, love the Lord, have a seeking heart, and are present in every meeting. Yet they do not know what their use is in the Lord's hand. Not only are they unable to tell, but the fact is that their usefulness has not been manifested. What is the reason for this?

The problem is in not loving the Lord absolutely, not consecrating oneself thoroughly, not abandoning one's future, not allowing one's self to be broken, and not experiencing the dealing of the flesh. If someone truly loved the Lord, completely consecrated himself, abandoned his future, and received the breaking and dealing, the Christ in him would be able to gain a place and an outlet to be expressed. At such a time, whether he senses it or not, his function would be manifested. Forgive me for saying that in the church today very few are called, very few are useful, very few can make a difference, very few can serve, and very few can be used by the Lord. The only reason and the greatest reason is that we are not absolute in loving the Lord and we do not completely hand ourselves over to Him, consecrating ourselves to Him, renouncing our future, and receiving the real breaking and dealing.

If we all would earnestly exercise ourselves in these five matters—loving the Lord absolutely, consecrating ourselves thoroughly, giving up our future, allowing our natural man to be broken, and letting our flesh be dealt with—then Christ would be able to have an outlet for His life to be lived out through us little by little. In this way we will have the assurance that one day we will become useful in the Lord's hands. Today the greatest reason for not knowing whether or not we are useful in the Lord's hands is that we do not practice these five items. We do not practice to love the Lord absolutely, to consecrate ourselves, to give up our future, to be dealt with, or to be broken. Our self still remains and still is preserved. Hence, we are zealous, yet we do not serve; we attend meetings, yet we are not useful; and we constantly meet together, but our functions are not clearly manifested. In many cases, it is not clearly manifested among us who are elders, who are deacons, or who are teachers.

Often when we, the workers, have gone to the churches to help them in appointing elders, after examining all the names of the brothers—studying them and praying for them—we could not find one who can be an elder. It seemed that they were all about the same; Brother A was about the same as Brother B, Brother B was about the same as Brother C, and Brother C was about the same as Brother D. They were all about the same. We could hardly find one who had the capacity to be an elder or had the function of a deacon. They all loved the Lord, they all were zealous and seeking, and they all regularly attended the meetings, yet they could not be made deacons or elders because the life in them did not clearly manifest their function.

We must see that every saved one is a person whom the Lord would use. The Lord's life is a serving life, and the Lord's life comes into us so that we can serve. However, our ability to serve is often not manifested. What is the reason for this? The reason is that the capacity to serve, which is inherent in the life within us, has not been developed. If because of the Lord's love, all of us would once again submit ourselves, consecrate ourselves, give up our future, and be broken and dealt with, in less than a year many brothers and sisters among us would be manifested as called ones, as workers, as elders, as deacons, and as those who engage in business, making money solely for the Lord. All the problems lie in the fact that the serving life within us cannot gain a place and has no way to grow. In such a situation, encouragement, teaching, and exhortation are all useless. Rather, what we need is to allow the life within us to find an outlet so that it can be released.

A certain brother who belonged to a wealthy family had followed the Lord for a long time and had also consecrated himself, but the function of life, the serving life, in him had not been manifested. In the spring of 1948, about the time of the Chinese New Year, I arrived at Ku-lang-yu, and the brothers arranged for me to stay in that brother's house. He had a huge Western style house that was quite magnificent, and the hospitality given to me was excellent. However, the most painful thing to me was that I had no one with whom to fellowship while I was staying there. If it were not for the fact that the Lord's grace had been constituted into me over the years, I probably would have become lifeless.

Within every cell of this brother's being was money, and all that he thought about was money. Sometimes he would take me for a little walk on the mountain, and on the way he would ask me many questions that he himself probably knew I would not be able to answer. How could you talk with such a person who was altogether living in money? Nevertheless, since he was the host and I was a guest, it would have been impolite to not answer his questions, so I had to answer something, though I knew that it was altogether useless. The crucial point of this story is that from that time on, at least a few times in my prayers I asked the Lord to remember that brother. I said, "Lord, this brother received Your servants and maidservants. He received me, and he also received some of the serving sisters. Lord, You must visit him. You must do a work of grace in him." Of course, any worker would naturally offer such a prayer without being exhorted to do so. That brother was saved, was pursuing the Lord, was interested in spiritual things, and also had no problem in the church life, but the big problem was that he had fallen into money and had become a money depository. Thus, the life of Christ in him was restricted. Therefore, although he was a saved one and was interested in spiritual things, the serving life could not be released through him.

A sacrifice that was to be presented to God first had to be brought to the altar, then it had to be slaughtered, cut into pieces, skinned, dealt with in various ways, and then finally burned by fire and offered to God. Therefore, all the dealings came after it was brought for consecration. In other words, our consecration may be considered the basis of the Lord's dealings with us. Why is this? According to simple reasoning, the Lord should have begun to deal with us immediately after we were saved so that He could begin to live Himself out through us more and more, yet many of us did not consent or agree to this. Since the Lord never forces us to do anything, He tries to draw us and move us to consecrate ourselves and say, "O Lord, I accept Your dealings and Your breaking." Such a response from us is our consecration; our consecration is our response.

Genuine consecration is to let God work in us. It is not that we work for God, as most people think. Genuine consecration is to let God work in us. It is not for us to work for the Lord. Many people think that after they have consecrated themselves, they have to work for the Lord. Little do they know that consecration is to allow the Lord to work in them, that is, to allow the Lord to carry out the work of dealing with them. Through our consecration the Lord receives the right and gets a response so that He can begin to work in us. Therefore, first comes consecration and then the dealings follow. Of course, sometimes there are exceptions. Sometimes the Lord may want to gain someone, yet this one refuses to consecrate himself. The Lord wants to win him, yet he refuses to say yes. The Lord wants to work in him, yet he would not go along and would not let Him do the work. Then what should the Lord do? The Lord has to raise up environments to deal a blow to him, his business, and to his health. This is still not the breaking but only a blow to force this one to have no alternative but to consecrate himself, to agree with the Lord, and to say yes to the Lord. The genuine dealing and breaking comes after consecration. Only after we have consecrated ourselves can we receive genuine dealing.

The blows mentioned above are outward. Even physical sickness is external. They are blows in the environment, not the dealings of the self within. After you have consecrated yourself, from then on the Lord begins to deal with your very self. We all know that Paul was dealt with not just once but for an extended period of time. He said that a thorn in the flesh was given to him. Concerning this thorn, he entreated the Lord three times that it might depart from him, yet the Lord did not remove it (2 Cor. 12:7-9). The Lord let the thorn remain in Paul, so the dealing never departed from Paul. Why is this? It was because he had not left his flesh yet. We must always remember that before we are transfigured and raptured, regardless of how much we have been dealt with by the Lord, our flesh remains unchanged. Thus, we need to live under His dealings daily.

It is quite a paradox that a person who has not been dealt with does not feel that he is fleshly. Every day his flesh is very active, yet he does not feel it. On the contrary, a person who is being dealt with every day has a strong sense that his flesh is present and that he is truly fleshly. It seems that if he speaks, he is fleshly, and if he does not speak, he is also fleshly. Regardless of what he does, he feels that he is fleshly. This experience is proper. The more we are dealt with, the more we will sense the flesh. Thus, we will submit ourselves to the Lord and say, "Lord, I am too poor." This is a good situation, a sweet situation. If you feel that after being dealt with once, it was a success—that your flesh has been broken and your naturalness has been purged—then you are being deceived. You have not been broken.

Even at the time Paul wrote the book of Philippians, he still said that he had not yet been perfected, he had not yet arrived, and he had not yet obtained. He was still pursuing and was still being dealt with (3:12-14). It is true that there are some who, even when they become old, are still useless in the Lord's hand. Why is this? It is because when they are old, they still would not be dealt with. We can never graduate from being dealt with.

HOW TO RECEIVE THE BREAKING

Concerning our receiving of the breaking, there are three points or stages to our experience. First the Lord's enlightenment, second our receiving or our executing, and third the coordination of the circumstances. What does breaking mean? Suppose there is a glass that was whole originally but now has been smashed into pieces. This is to be broken. This should be clear to all of us. Consider yourself. Your natural life, your temperament, your disposition, and your flesh all are whole. However, now that you have been saved, Christ's life has entered into you. That life needs to be released from your spirit, yet it has been surrounded. By what is it surrounded? It is surrounded by your natural life, your flesh, your temperament, and your disposition. All that you have surrounds the life of Christ, preventing it from being released. Therefore, all that you have in you that is whole needs to be broken. Only when all these things are broken can Christ's life be released.

First, God will shine His light in you to show you that all that you have, including your natural life, your flesh, your temper, and your disposition, are enemies of the life of Christ and are frustrations and limitations to the life of Christ. God will also show you that all these things have already been crucified because they are things rejected by God, they are enemies of God, and they are frustrations to the life of Christ. After you have seen such a light, immediately the Holy Spirit in you will come and execute this light in all matters big and small in your daily life. Before you saw this light, you had no feeling or sense of condemnation when you lost your temper and acted in a fleshly way, but now after seeing the light, the Holy Spirit in you executes this light with you. When you act in your natural life and lose your temper, the Holy Spirit gives you the sense that this is your flesh, your natural life, your self, and your temper, all of which should be condemned because they were already put to death on the cross. Then by the power of the Holy Spirit you condemn these things, executing the crucifixion over them. At this time, crucifixion is not merely an objective truth on the cross but a subjective experience in you. This is the putting to death of the practices of the body mentioned in Romans 8:13. This is also the death that causes the putting to death of Jesus to operate in us, as referred to in 2 Corinthians 4:11-12.

We know that the life of Christ has the element of death, and when this element passes through us, it does a killing work in us. This is similar to our blood cells, which have at least two functions. The first function is to kill the enemies of our body—the bacteria, and the second function is to simultaneously supply our body with the necessary nutrients. We saw this light a few years ago but did not speak about it because we did not have the boldness to say that in the life of Christ there is the effect of death. However, in our experience we gradually have become more and more clear about this. Recently we saw that Brother Andrew Murray also said the same thing. He said that in the life of Christ there is a killing power, an element of death, an effect of death.

Once the Holy Spirit has gained a place in us, He will lead us daily to put to death our natural life and our flesh. This putting to death, this killing, is the breaking. Furthermore, in order to help us, God also gives us the discipline of the Holy Spirit on the outside by arranging our circumstances so that He can work in us in a joint effort within and without. The life of Christ works on the inside while the circumstances work on the outside. When we have the desire to receive the breaking, immediately there is the coordination of the things on the inside and the outside, and the Holy Spirit begins to carry out the breaking work in us. However, if our heart's desire and our spirit do not go along with the Holy Spirit to execute the killing, then all the circumstances, regardless of how many there are, are of little use. The outward circumstances work in coordination with the Holy Spirit within us, and in between these two factors there is a third necessary factor—our receiving.

The Spirit is on the inside, the circumstances are on the outside, and in between these two we have to be the receiving ones, the executing ones. In this way, day by day and time after time, our natural life, our flesh, and our self will be broken. Eventually, when we are about to lose our temper, we will no longer be able to do it because we have been broken and have many wounds in us.

ABOUT THE AUTHOR

Witness Lee was born in 1905 in northern China and raised in a Christian family. At age 19 he was fully captured for Christ and immediately consecrated himself to preach the gospel for the rest of his life. Early in his service, he met Watchman Nee, a renowned preacher, teacher, and writer. Witness Lee labored together with Watchman Nee under his direction. In 1934 Watchman Nee entrusted Witness Lee with the responsibility for his publication operation, called the Shanghai Gospel Bookroom.

Prior to the Communist takeover in 1949, Witness Lee was sent by Watchman Nee and his other co-workers to Taiwan to ensure that the things delivered to them by the Lord would not be lost. Watchman Nee instructed Witness Lee to continue the former's publishing operation abroad as the Taiwan Gospel Bookroom, which has been publicly recognized as the publisher of Watchman Nee's works outside China. Witness Lee's work in Taiwan manifested the Lord's abundant blessing. From a mere 350 believers, newly fled from the mainland, the churches in Taiwan grew to 20,000 in five years.

In 1962 Witness Lee felt led of the Lord to come to the United States, settling in California. During his 35 years of service in the U.S., he ministered in weekly meetings and weekend conferences, delivering several thousand spoken messages. Much of his speaking has since been published as over 400 titles. Many of these have been translated into over fourteen languages. He gave his last public conference in February 1997 at the age of 91.

He leaves behind a prolific presentation of the truth in the Bible. His major work, *Life-study of the Bible,* comprises over 25,000 pages of commentary on every book of the Bible from the perspective of the believers' enjoyment and experience of God's divine life in Christ through the Holy Spirit. Witness Lee was the chief editor of a new translation of the New Testament into Chinese called the Recovery Version and directed the translation of the same into English. The Recovery Version also appears in a number of other languages. He provided an extensive body of footnotes, outlines, and spiritual cross references. A radio broadcast of his messages can be heard on Christian radio stations in the United States. In 1965 Witness Lee founded Living Stream Ministry, a non-profit corporation, located in Anaheim, California, which officially presents his and Watchman Nee's ministry.

Witness Lee's ministry emphasizes the experience of Christ as life and the practical oneness of the believers as the Body of Christ. Stressing the importance of attending to both these matters, he led the churches under his care to grow in Christian life and function. He was unbending in his conviction that God's goal is not narrow sectarianism but the Body of Christ. In time, believers began to meet simply as the church in their localities in response to this conviction. In recent years a number of new churches have been raised up in Russia and in many eastern European countries.

OTHER BOOKS PUBLISHED BY
Living Stream Ministry

Titles by Witness Lee:

Abraham—Called by God	978-0-7363-0359-0
The Experience of Life	978-0-87083-417-2
The Knowledge of Life	978-0-87083-419-6
The Tree of Life	978-0-87083-300-7
The Economy of God	978-0-87083-415-8
The Divine Economy	978-0-87083-268-0
God's New Testament Economy	978-0-87083-199-7
The World Situation and God's Move	978-0-87083-092-1
Christ vs. Religion	978-0-87083-010-5
The All-inclusive Christ	978-0-87083-020-4
Gospel Outlines	978-0-87083-039-6
Character	978-0-87083-322-9
The Secret of Experiencing Christ	978-0-87083-227-7
The Life and Way for the Practice of the Church Life	978-0-87083-785-2
The Basic Revelation in the Holy Scriptures	978-0-87083-105-8
The Crucial Revelation of Life in the Scriptures	978-0-87083-372-4
The Spirit with Our Spirit	978-0-87083-798-2
Christ as the Reality	978-0-87083-047-1
The Central Line of the Divine Revelation	978-0-87083-960-3
The Full Knowledge of the Word of God	978-0-87083-289-5
Watchman Nee—A Seer of the Divine Revelation ...	978-0-87083-625-1

Titles by Watchman Nee:

How to Study the Bible	978-0-7363-0407-8
God's Overcomers	978-0-7363-0433-7
The New Covenant	978-0-7363-0088-9
The Spiritual Man • 3 volumes	978-0-7363-0269-2
Authority and Submission	978-0-7363-0185-5
The Overcoming Life	978-1-57593-817-2
The Glorious Church	978-0-87083-745-6
The Prayer Ministry of the Church	978-0-87083-860-6
The Breaking of the Outer Man and the Release ...	978-1-57593-955-1
The Mystery of Christ	978-1-57593-954-4
The God of Abraham, Isaac, and Jacob	978-0-87083-932-0
The Song of Songs	978-0-87083-872-9
The Gospel of God • 2 volumes	978-1-57593-953-7
The Normal Christian Church Life	978-0-87083-027-3
The Character of the Lord's Worker	978-1-57593-322-1
The Normal Christian Faith	978-0-87083-748-7
Watchman Nee's Testimony	978-0-87083-051-8

Available at
Christian bookstores, or contact Living Stream Ministry
2431 W. La Palma Ave. • Anaheim, CA 92801
1-800-549-5164 • www.livingstream.com